Eat It!

Eat It!

The Most Sustainable Diet and Workout Ever Made:

Burn Fat, Get Strong, and Enjoy Your Favorite Foods Guilt Free

Jordan Syatt and Michael Vacanti

Foreword by Gary Vaynerchuk

HARPER WAVE

An Imprint of HarperCollins*Publishers*

HarperCollins books may be purchased for educational, business, or sales promotional use. For information, please email the Special Markets Department at SPsales@harpercollins.com.

FIRST EDITION

All images unless otherwise credited are © Gabriela Ioachim
The appendix image on page 207 is © Michael Vacanti, On the Regimen

Designed by Bonni Leon-Berman

Library of Congress Cataloging-in-Publication Data has been applied for.

ISBN 978-0-06-301500-5

22 23 24 25 26   LSC   10 9 8 7 6 5 4 3 2 1

For all the highly palatable foods, without which this book would not be possible. Or needed.

Contents

Part III: Lift It!

Foreword

When I started training with Mike and Jordan, I was thirty-eight years old and had been struggling to win the fitness game for fifteen years. I'm a strong believer in the power of DNA and innate skills, and I'm grateful to have a ton of natural ability. I'm amazing at business. I can rally an audience around any idea that I believe in. Fitness, on the other hand, just doesn't come naturally to me. It's not about the effort—I'm obsessed with hard work. I grew my family's retail wine business from $3 million to $60 million within five years of taking over the company. I started a media empire with my brother, AJ, that now employs more than eight hundred people. I will never stop hustling, but I could not get my ass to the gym or control myself when I saw a tray of chicken wings before I met these guys.

Mike and Jordan were my trainers for a collective seven years—Mike the first two years, Jordan for three, then they alternated—and I was a fucking mess when we started. I knew nothing about nutrition. I was working and traveling 24/7 with zero time to think about food or exercise. And my biggest obstacle: I believed that I suck at this whole fitness thing.

So, I was amazed by how well their program worked for me. By the end of our time together I was able to deadlift 315 pounds after never picking up a barbell in my life. I've maintained my goal weight. I can open a refrigerator, or a restaurant menu, and eat without guilt—even when it's something "unhealthy." I can keep up with my kids without feeling like an old man. I can lift a heavy bag from an overhead compartment without worrying about what it will do to my back. I am proof that their approach works even on someone who never felt like a natural in the gym.

I understand my experience will be different from yours. Reading a book by two trainers is not the same as working with them every day for years. But I still believe there is a high likelihood that *Eat It!* will be the breakthrough you've been looking for because Mike and Jordan's program is so powerful. It works because these guys set you up for the long game. Their expertise is backed by a genuine desire to help people, and that shines through in everything they do. The end result—the book you're holding—is equal parts compassion and tough love, and I believe this fitness program will stick with you even if others did not. It did for me.

These guys also have an amazing ability to call bullshit on the misinformation around fitness that holds so many people back. They point out the crap, then they take the time to teach you how nutrition actually works so you can make smarter choices. It's overwhelming to think about the sheer level of education Mike and Jordan brought into my life. They didn't just tell me what to eat. They *taught me how to eat* in a way that makes my body and mind feel great. They didn't just give me an exercise routine. They helped me see why strength training makes sense for everyday life—and I'm a huge commonsense guy. Who the heck wants to work out their legs? But I do it because I understand how useful it is, especially when I'm older, to have strong leg muscles.

Strength training has a tremendous impact on my day-to-day life in a way I never would have imagined.

Mike and Jordan also opened my eyes to one of the biggest mistakes people make with their nutrition: that you can't outwork your mouth. We'd like to think we can eat like crap if we just hit the gym hard, but the math doesn't work out that way. We usually eat more calories than we realize, and we never burn as many calories working out as we think.

And one of the biggest reasons Mike and Jordan's program works is because they don't demonize the misstep. If you eat a whole pizza or a bucket of ice cream after six days of sticking to your calorie goals, they never make you feel like you've fucked up. Even if you spend a month eating that way, you still didn't fuck up. And Mike and Jordan have seen me do a lot of things that could count as fucking up.

There was the day at the Mets game when I ate an entire catering tray of BBQ baked beans and was up five pounds the next morning.

There are the dozens of wings I eat during my fantasy baseball draft every year, bones and all.

There was the time I discovered that I could manipulate the scale by pressing my big toe against the wall when I step on it . . . and the two months I used that trick to eat like shit and send them accountability photos of my fake weight. By the time I cracked and told them about my toe scam, I'd gained seven pounds. But they didn't consider it a setback. They suggested I stop lying to myself, and to them, but they didn't treat me like I'd done something wrong. We just kept moving forward—because they're always about the long game.

You are in incredible hands with Mike and Jordan. They are constantly learning, and you and I get to benefit from the curiosity and passion that they bring to their craft. They care deeply about helping people live their best lives. I think the ingredients of who they are, how they communicate, and the care and empathy they bring to fitness—an area of life that so many of us struggle with—will bring lasting change to your world.

—*Gary Vaynerchuk*

Part I
Believe It!

1

You Can't F*ck This Up

Have you ever gone out to dinner, eaten enough chips and guac to feed a family of twelve, then worried because you thought you ruined your progress?

Have you ever been sick, injured, or traveling and had to skip a workout or even an entire week of workouts? And did you feel guilty or nervous that you messed everything up?

Listen. You can't screw this up.

We're gonna say it again. Keep reading.

You cannot screw this up.

We don't care if you blew past your calories by an extra 3,000. You didn't mess up. We don't care if you missed one workout or two workouts or a month of workouts. You didn't mess up. We don't care if you had an entire box of Cinnamon Toast Crunch, six slices of pizza, four pints of Ben & Jerry's, and a basketful of chocolate turtles. That's definitely an odd combination of food choices. But you didn't mess up.

Because here's the part most "fitness gurus" get wrong: the only way to mess up is to stop altogether. Give up. Quit. Say you're done.

See, most people use "I messed up" as an excuse to keep

messing up. To stay off track. They let one bad meal turn into a day, then a week, then a month, then years. But that's nonsense. And as of this moment it's not a valid excuse. Because you can't screw this up. It's impossible. As long as you get right back on track, you're going to keep making progress.

This fitness thing? It's supposed to be fun. It's supposed to make you confident, happy, and healthy. It's not a competition. There is no finish line at which you need to arrive to achieve your goals. There is no rush. You're playing the long game here. It's for life, not seven or twenty-one or thirty days. This is forever. And when you're playing forever, you can't screw up.

Before we dive into calories, protein, cardio, strength training, supplements, insulin, your thyroid, or anything else fitness gurus love to Instagram about, we need to discuss the most important precursor to your success: your mindset.

The hardest part of losing weight, getting stronger, and becoming healthier isn't figuring out what to eat or finding the perfect workout plan or optimizing your macros. The hardest part is cultivating a mindset that allows you to believe in your ability to succeed *and* prevents you from quitting when you aren't losing weight as quickly as you would like.

The truth is, your progress will be slower than you want. And—we aren't going to sugarcoat this—it will be a difficult process. But as long as you don't quit, you will succeed. It's not a question of "if," only a matter of "when."

The deciding factor isn't the latest "super food" nonsense

like goji berries or raspberry ketones, it's whether you're willing to keep trying when the easier choice is to quit altogether.

So if you're ready to give this a shot, we're ready to help.

The First Step

A woman emailed us saying she felt anxious about getting started and needed some advice.

"I'm forty-nine years old," she said. "I'm severely overweight. Beyond out of shape. And I haven't exercised in years. How does someone like me start? I can't even do knee push-ups. I'm hopeless. Can you help?"

"What about walking?" we asked.

"Walking works!"

Don't let the illusion of complexity fool you into thinking you don't know where to start or that you can't do anything worthwhile. You can. You can always walk. You can always stretch. You can always drink more water. You can always eat more fruits and vegetables. You can always do *something*. And as long as you do something, and do it consistently, no matter how simple it may seem, you will make progress.

There's a fallacy about health and fitness: that if you can't do a comprehensive, hour-long workout it's not worth working out at all. That's nonsense. Something is always better than nothing. We don't care if it's a 15-minute circuit, 5-minute walk, or a 10-second hamstring stretch. Action leads to motivation. Not the other way around. Doing one small thing will act as the catalyst for you to do it again. And again. And again. From those small, consistent actions you'll make progress. From that progress you'll get more confidence. And with that confidence you'll take more action. And so the cycle continues.

Stop wasting time looking for the "best" workout program or the "perfect" diet. They don't exist. And the more time you spend searching, the longer you'll be disappointed with your lack of progress. You're never going to feel 100 percent ready to begin. You will always have a reason not to start. And there will always be something more important to do. You will mess up. And you will make mistakes. Don't let that prevent you from getting started. Because just like no one ever got skinny from eating one salad, no one ever got fat from eating one doughnut. Progress, in either direction, takes time and consistency. And the only way to fail is if you quit altogether.

Not sure what to do? That's why you're reading this book, silly. We're going to take away all the guesswork so there are no questions and there's zero ambiguity. We're going to give you a step-by-step plan that shows you exactly how to lose fat, get stronger, and live a healthier, happier life. Just make a promise to us and, more important, yourself: you are going to take the first step. Today. Right now. Even if it's going for a walk around the block. Or drinking an extra glass of water. Just begin. Your weight may not drop the first week, or even the first two weeks, but you'll feel better. You'll have more energy. And you'll be proud of yourself for making better decisions. You don't need to hit your goals perfectly every day. You won't. The goal isn't to be perfect. The goal is to be consistent. And as long as you're consistently trying to improve, you will make progress.

You Know That Friend Who Can Eat Whatever They Want without Gaining Weight?

They're the worst, right? Kidding. Sort of. First, let's set the scene:

It's 8:00 p.m. on a Friday. You're out to dinner with a few friends from work and you're stoked because you've been on point with your diet all week, but now you're getting anxious because you don't want to ruin your progress. You also don't want to be "that person" who refuses to eat or drink anything unhealthy. You want to enjoy yourself with everyone, but the ever-present fear of ruining all your progress in one fell swoop is getting stronger.

As if it wasn't already bad enough, your friend who can eat whatever they want without gaining weight is happily enjoying a plateful of french fries while downing their second margarita without a care in the world.

How can they eat whatever they want and still look like that? you ask yourself. *It's ridiculous. I so much as make eye contact with a french fry and immediately look like a beluga whale.*

Should you tell everyone you're full so you don't have to eat? Should you say you aren't feeling well so you can go home early and get out of the situation altogether? Or maybe you should just say "screw it" and eat whatever you want, because you were perfect all week and you're tired of being so damn strict with your diet.

None of the options sound good, but you see all your friends eating and drinking and enjoying themselves, so eventually you say "screw it" and go all out. You have several margaritas, entirely too many dinner rolls, a basket of french fries, three tacos, and a full ice cream sundae to yourself. When you get home you aren't hungry, yet you make a super necessary pit stop in the kitchen for a few chocolate chip cookies and two oatmeal cream pies for good measure.

You make your way to bed feeling uncomfortably full, disappointed in your lack of self-control, and resentful of your friend who can eat whatever they want without gaining weight while you just undid all your hard work from the past week.

Saturday morning you wake up late and skip your workout because why bother? You already screwed up last night, so you might as well make yourself some pancakes with syrup and whipped cream today, then get back on track on Monday. You spend the rest of the weekend eating as much as you possibly can of all the "bad" foods you aren't going to allow yourself to eat during the week.

On Monday morning you weigh in, disgusted with yourself, and swear to never eat another carb for the rest of your life. You decide to fast the entire day so you can "undo" the damage from the weekend and lose the weight as quickly as possible.

Of course, when you're at the office you see your friend

who can eat whatever they want without gaining weight inhaling a Hershey's chocolate bar after lunch.

What the hell!? you shriek in your head. *Here I am starving myself all day while they go around eating chocolate and looking amazing without gaining an ounce of fat? It's not fair!*

Listen. If this sounds the least bit familiar it's because it happens more than you could imagine. More people struggle with this than you think. The issue, however, isn't a matter of fairness. The issue is your perception of what's actually happening.

You know your friend who can eat whatever they want without gaining weight? What you didn't realize at dinner is they didn't finish the entire plate of french fries. And instead of having a whole dessert to themself, they had a few bites, then stopped eating once they were full.

When they got home they had a glass of water and went to bed so they could wake up hydrated and get their workout in. They stayed on track with their regular schedule, and they knew they didn't ruin any of their progress the night before, so they didn't feel the urge to stuff themselves all weekend.

They woke up on Monday morning and had a great breakfast of oatmeal, a couple of eggs, and some fruit. For lunch they had a big salad with lots of fresh vegetables and grilled chicken on top. For dessert they packed a Hershey's chocolate bar, which you conveniently spotted them eating after they finished their salad. This led you to jump to conclusions and get angry that they can eat whatever they want without gaining weight while you "need to starve yourself" in order to make progress.

See, the issue isn't your friend, your metabolism, your age, your gender, or your genetics. The issue is your relationship with food. The issue is your all-or-nothing mentality. And the issue is, above all else, your lack of consistency. The moment you thought you screwed up, you justified eating as much as you possibly could for the rest of the weekend, which only made you feel worse about yourself and your lack of progress.

It would be like getting a flat tire and then proceeding to slash your other three. It doesn't make sense. It only perpetuates the problem. And from this moment forward, you won't be doing it anymore. You're ending the cycle right here, right now, once and for all. All you need to do is understand *you can't screw this up*. You can't. It's impossible. Remember, you're never more than one bite away from getting right back on track. And as long as you stay consistent (not perfect) and get back to doing what you know is right, you will make progress and achieve your goals.

Just don't quit.

Last Words Before We Start

It can't be said enough, so let us make this abundantly clear.

Consistently good is infinitely better than inconsistently perfect. This is not our way of encouraging you to be lazy or make a half-assed effort. Rather it's our way of:

1. **Getting you to stop beating yourself up after eating half a pizza or a whole box of powdered doughnuts.** Ideally, you won't make that a regular habit. But on the off chance you have a bad day and eat more than you should, it's not going to make or break your progress. So relax. Stop beating yourself up. Enjoy it. Then get back on track.

2. **Encouraging you to stop wasting time waiting for the "perfect" moment to commit to your goals.** It's never going to come. You will always be busy. You will always have other responsibilities and obligations. You will rarely (if ever) think you're 100 percent ready to dive in. But the longer you wait for the timing to be "perfect," the longer you delay your chance to achieve your goals. Stop waiting. Start now.

We'd rather you hit your nutrition 80 percent than 100 percent. Because at 80 percent you can enjoy yourself without obsessing over every single calorie. Your progress will be slower but more sustainable and enjoyable. Being 100 percent on point isn't perfect; it's prison.

2

Set Habits That Will Keep You in This Long Term

The not-so-sexy truth about fat loss is it isn't easy. It isn't quick. It isn't fun or glamorous. Fat loss sucks. We realize we could sell more copies of this book by saying it's quick and easy. But that's not the truth, and we aren't here to lie to you.

There are certainly ways to make fat loss suck less and be more sustainable (which we'll discuss later on). You don't need to eliminate your favorite foods, you're absolutely able to lose fat without starving yourself, you don't need an overpriced diarrhea tea that's marketed as a "detox," and you can 100 percent lose fat while having fun and living life.

But the mental side of fat loss is what most people overlook. It never goes as quickly as you want. You regularly feel like you're messing up. You often doubt yourself and your ability to stay on track. You regularly feel like you're missing out on social events and struggle to find the balance between being strict enough to achieve your goals and flexible enough to enjoy yourself.

The good news is all these struggles are normal. We all go through them. And with enough time, effort, and patience you can come out on the other side, fully understanding how to stay lean year-round without having these feelings again. The difference between those who succeed and those who don't lies in your ability to fail, get back up, and try again. Because you will go off track. You will make mistakes. You will have days and weeks and months that don't go your way.

That's okay. You will succeed. We promise. Just as long as you're willing to keep getting back up and trying again and again. Because the only way to guarantee failure is to quit. So don't quit. Grit your teeth. Stand back up. And keep going. You've got this.

In Chapter 8 we'll give you practical strategies for staying on track with your nutrition. But before we get into dieting specifics we need to chat about motivation. Because the question isn't whether you'll stay motivated forever. You won't. Not because you don't want to, but because it's impossible to stay motivated all the time for anything, regardless of how much you want it.

In the same way it's unrealistic to expect to be happy all day, every day, it's equally unrealistic to expect to be motivated all day, every day. Motivation is a feeling. An emotion. The more you search for it and try to find it in unsuspecting places, the more it will evade you. You might have moments in which you think you've finally trapped it. But just like trying to trap water in your cupped hands, motivation will slip between the cracks in your fingers until, once again, your hands are empty.

The question isn't whether you'll stay motivated. The question is whether or not you'll do what you say you want to do regardless of whether you're motivated. That's not a feeling or emotion. That's your word. Your integrity. Your bond. You will not stay forever motivated to do everything you want. None of us will. But the difference between those who succeed and those who don't lies in your willingness to hold up your end of the bargain. Are you willing to make the decision to do what is right rather than what is easy, and make the hard decisions that will make you proud rather than the easy decisions that will make you comfortable?

Stop looking for motivation. Start asking yourself if you're ready to commit to achieving your goals. There is tremendous power in knowing and understanding you will not always be motivated. The only way to achieve your goals is to stick to your plan even, and especially, when you aren't motivated to do it.

The mindset strategies we're about to share are tools that we, and our clients, have found to be the most effective for staying on track when you want to quit. It will take time to adopt them as true habits, so be kind to yourself. This is a journey. To start, just read. Let the ideas sink in. Keep them in mind and lean on them as you implement your nutrition and workout plans. Over time, they'll become habits your brain turns to so you can do what is right even when you aren't motivated to do it.

Nothing Matters Unless You Believe You Can Do This

The reason most people never achieve their fitness goals is because they don't actually believe they can. There is a voice in their head—whether it's their own or someone else's—that tells them they're bound to fail. They feel like they shouldn't even bother trying, because what's the point if it's not going to work anyway? It's suffocating, overwhelming, and if you don't learn how to silence that voice, you're marching headfirst into a losing battle.

This book is to help you silence that voice. To eliminate it from your life once and for all. And to create a new voice that allows you to realize you *can* do this. A voice that pushes and encourages you to take action and never quit. Because each and every action you take toward your goals, no matter how big or small, is proof that you believe you can do this.

We know this might sound a little hippie-dippie, but it's true. There is a staggering amount of research showing that people who believe in their ability to succeed are drastically more likely to achieve their goals than those who don't.[*] There's even a term for it: *self-efficacy*, and the higher your self-efficacy (aka the more you believe in yourself), the greater your chances of success.

Think about it like this: if you don't believe you can suc-

---

[*] Jacinda B. Roach et al., "Using Self-Efficacy to Predict Weight Loss among Young Adults," *Journal of the American Dietetic Association*, Elsevier, October 8, 2004, https://www.sciencedirect.com/science/article/abs/pii /S0002822303010721.

ceed, why would you wake up early and go to the gym when you could stay in bed? Why would you spend money on a gym membership when you could spend it on something else? Why would you take the time to learn how to improve your nutrition or exercise technique? Why would you do any of this if you didn't think it was going to work? You wouldn't. Which is why no matter where you are starting from—whether you want to lose 20 pounds or 200 pounds—you need to believe in your ability to succeed. And, fortunately, you've already proven you do believe in yourself (at least a little bit) because you're reading this book. So keep going. You've got this.

Sometimes when we find folks struggling with their self-efficacy, we challenge them to consider our lottery ticket analogy. Let's say we told you that if you spent $10,000 on lottery tickets today you would have a 99 percent chance of winning $1 million. $10,000 is a huge investment, but if you knew you had a 99 percent chance of winning, you'd buy them immediately because you know you're almost certainly going to win. On the other hand, let's say we told you that if you spent $10,000 on lottery tickets today, you would have a 1 percent chance of winning $1 million. You probably wouldn't do it because you don't actually believe you're going to win.

The same concept applies to fitness (and all aspects of life, really). The more you believe in your ability to succeed, the more likely you are to put the requisite time, energy, and effort into doing what is necessary to achieve your goals. It's a self-fulfilling prophecy. And, fortunately, in the case of your health and fitness, it isn't a gamble; it's science. If you improve your nutrition, eat appropriate portions, exercise consistently, sleep well, and stay hydrated, you will absolutely, without a shadow of a doubt succeed.

Remember, you don't need to be perfect. You just need to be consistent. You shouldn't expect to hit your nutrition 100 percent of the time. And you shouldn't expect to work out 365 days per year. It's unrealistic, and the more pressure you put on yourself, the less likely you are to succeed because you know it's not going to happen.

The question is . . . will you be consistent?

If you make the investment of your time and energy, and believe in yourself, you will achieve your goals. You will lose body fat. You will get stronger. You will get more defined. You will be healthier, happier, and more confident. You will be physically and mentally stronger than you ever thought possible. It's not a question of "if," only a matter of "when."

Stop Waiting and Take Action

"How do I get motivated?" is the most common question we get asked. There are nearly two hundred million search results for that exact question on Google (seriously, go check). And it makes sense because motivation is something each and every one of us struggles with and wishes we had more of.

Candidly, if there were a pill or powder or supplement for sale that could increase your motivation, we would be first in line to buy it. Unfortunately, that's not how motivation works. And the only way to get motivated is to do the thing you aren't motivated to do.

Let's say, for example, you have a child. A boy. We'll call him Charlie. If Charlie came home from school and told you he wasn't going to do his homework because he "just wasn't motivated," hopefully you'd say, "Tough shit, Charlie, get to work."

Same goes for you.

If you're waiting to get motivated before you decide to work out or improve your nutrition or get more sleep or drink more water, you're going to be waiting a long time. See, most people think motivation is the first step in the process. It isn't. And thinking you're just going to "get motivated" out of nowhere is a pipe dream.

First, you need to take action. Even (and especially) when you aren't motivated to do it. Maybe it's walking 5 minutes per day. Maybe it's drinking a glass of water before you eat. Maybe it's having one piece of fruit before 10:00 a.m. every day. Maybe it's counting your calories one day each week.

We don't care what it is. We just care that you pick something productive and do it. Because this equation begins with action (not motivation). From your action you get results. And from your results you get motivated. And with that motivation you take more action. And so the cycle continues.

But it all starts with action. So stop waiting until you're motivated. And stop breaking promises to yourself. If you made a promise to a friend or family member, you'd keep it, so let's make a habit of keeping the promises you make to yourself, as well. Make the decision to do something (no matter how small) every day that will get you closer to achieving your goals. And do it. Even when you don't want to. Because just like Charlie needs to get to work . . . so do you.

Client Spotlight

Keep Good Company and Stay Focused

When Jenny started her fitness journey with Mike, she'd been overweight her whole life. She shared, "I'd been trying to lose weight for a long time, but I just didn't know how. It is so confusing when you try to look up advice online. There are contradictions everywhere. I was so overwhelmed that I couldn't do anything."

Jenny got past the noise and lost 35 pounds in 8 months. And even more important than mastering her nutrition or workout strategies? Finally believing she could do it.

Two factors helped keep Jenny's self-efficacy strong: a solid support system and remembering that she can't mess this up.

On having a support system

"You need people to go to if you're having a bad day; people who aren't going to give you a hard time when you say 'no' to going out to eat or when you're not getting your usual treats at the movies.

"I got a lot of criticism from people when I first started doing this. I wasn't expecting that. I kept hearing, 'That seems hard, why are you doing that?' or 'That's not how to lose weight—just stop eating carbs, or just do this or that.' Then, when I started seeing results, those same people asked me how I did it.

"It's a big adjustment for everyone around you—not just for you. Having a few close people to back me up was a huge help when other friends doubted my choices."

Jenny's experience demonstrates the factors that build grit. A difficult goal becomes even harder when others are trying to bring you down. Make sure you have a few people who get what you're trying to do—and who believe in you, too. Bonus points if they share similar goals.

On realizing she can't mess this up

"There were so many times I wanted to give up. It felt like too much. I was tired. I wasn't having fun. On really bad days, when

I felt I was totally off track, I'd reach out to Mike, and it felt like I was confessing all my bad choices. But his response always surprised me. He'd just say, 'Yep! That's part of the process. It happens to everyone. It's not actually a mistake.'

"I never thought I could do this. It sounds so weird for me to even say that I count calories or that I lift weights. I am so laid-back, they're just not things I ever would have done. But having that one message on repeat, 'You can't mess this up,' finally helped me believe I could succeed. It stopped me from doubting myself and from comparing myself to others. It kept other people's criticisms from getting into my head. I was able to just focus."

Consistency Goals Are Better Than Weight Loss Goals

We're not saying it's bad to have a weight loss goal. For example, a goal of losing an average of 1 pound per week is totally fine and works for many people (ourselves included). However, if you choose to have a weight loss goal, it's critical that you understand your weight loss won't be linear. Even if your nutrition is "perfect" and you never miss a workout, the scale will not go down every day or even every week. The scale is not logical and measures far more than simply fat gain and loss (more on that in Chapter 3).

This is why we care more about your consistency than your weight. See, most people start by making a monthly weight loss goal as a way to stay motivated. This is great, except for the fact that your motivation is now being derived from something you can't fully control. And when (not if) the time comes in which you don't hit your monthly weight loss goal, will you say "screw it" and quit?

If yes, then don't make a monthly weight loss goal. Instead, make a monthly consistency goal using the 80/20 rule. And you know what? Even if you wouldn't quit if you didn't hit the monthly weight loss goal, you should still make a monthly consistency goal. Because you have control over your consistency. It's objective. You either hit your calories 80 percent of the time or you don't. You either hit your protein 80 percent of the time or you don't. You either hit your workouts 80 percent of the time or you don't. There's no room for messing with numbers or screwing with the data. You were either consistent or you weren't.

If you want to make consistent progress, you need to be ruthlessly consistent for at least 24–26 days each month. And if you track your consistency even half as meticulously as so many people obsessively track their weight, you'll be able to track your progress and objectively analyze where you can improve.

Here's what consistency looks like:

1. Get a 30-day calendar. Do not rely on your phone or computer calendar. Get a physical calendar that you can put in your office, kitchen, bathroom, or wherever you know you'll be every day.
2. Keep a red marker and a black marker handy.

3. Do these three things every day:

    I. Weigh yourself. This is just for data-tracking purposes. What you actually weigh from day to day is insignificant on its own. (More on this in Chapter 3.)

    II. Hit your nutrition goals. (We'll explain your nutrition guidelines in Part 2.)

    III. Do your workout, if you have one planned. (We'll outline your workout program in Part 3.)

On the days you do all three things, mark the calendar with a red X. On the days you don't, mark the calendar with a black O. Your goal is to get a red X 24–26 days each month. That comes to about 80 percent consistency.

Be precise with this. If your daily calorie range is 1,900–2,100 and you ate 2,150 calories, mark the black O and move on. Clients often ask us why they need to mark an O if they ate only slightly more than their daily calorie allowance. They ask us if that means they failed and if they should reduce their calories the following day.

No, you did not fail because you ate slightly more than you were supposed to. And you should not eat less the following day to "make up for it." The reason you need to mark an O even if you ate only slightly more than your daily allowance is simple: because you need to track your consistency honestly and objectively. If you hit your calories, you were consistent. If you didn't hit your calories, you weren't consistent. Simple as that.

Marking an O doesn't mean you failed. It means you ate more than you planned to, and you can get right back on track tomorrow. Truth be told, we not only expect you to have Os on your calendar but we also want you to. If you hit your calories every single day with 100 percent consistency for six months straight, you probably had a pretty boring six months. We would rather you be 80 percent consistent than 100 percent consistent because at 80 percent you can have fun, enjoy your favorite foods, and not have to worry about being "perfect."

While we don't expect your nutrition to be perfect, we do expect you to be 100 percent honest with your consistency calendar. The point in being so exact is to ensure you have accurate and reliable data. Then, when you're measuring progress over months, or even the whole year, you can compare it to your track record. If you didn't make reasonable progress over a long stretch of time, check the numbers: Were you 80 percent consistent throughout that period?

If you were not consistent 80 percent of the time, you have your answer. You haven't earned the right to be frustrated with your progress if you were consistent, say, 70 percent of the time. That's a C minus. Sure, you passed the class, but you can't expect A plus results from C minus effort. So just use that data to help keep you moving forward. Tomorrow is a new day to start a solid streak of 80 percent Xs.

Don't Compare Your Chapter 1 to Someone Else's Chapter 15

Every time we say, "Don't compare yourself to others," someone says, "Thanks, assholes, but that's easier said than done."

And they're right. It is. And, in fairness, comparing yourself to others isn't inherently bad.

Comparison is the reason hundreds of people have beaten the four-minute mile since Roger Bannister ran it in 1954, back when it was thought to be physically impossible. Comparison is one of the reasons having a workout partner can help you stay consistent even when you don't want to go to the gym. Comparison, used appropriately, can motivate you, push you, drive you to be better, hold you accountable, and help you believe in your ability to succeed.

But used inappropriately, comparison is crippling. It can demotivate you, cause you to feel insecure and to second-guess your abilities and decisions, and give you a reason to justify not trying at all. That's what needs to stop. This is where you need to consciously set your boundaries.

Stop tearing yourself apart because some fitness model has perfectly symmetrical six-pack abs and you don't. Stop calling yourself fat because an "influencer" eating 700 calories a day has a thigh gap wider than the Pacific Ocean while your thighs rub against each other (like a normal human being's). Stop feeling like a failure because your body doesn't look like the girl on Instagram who has a fake butt and tiny Photoshopped waist.

By all means, compare yourself to yourself. Use it as motivation to get leaner, stronger, and more athletic and to build a healthy relationship with food. But don't waste your time or energy comparing yourself to a sea of strangers you don't know and have never met, and whose lives you have literally zero context to outside of what they choose to share on social media.

Set a Personal Rule: Holidays Are Holidays

Many people stress about losing their progress while on vacation, over Thanksgiving, Christmas, their birthday, or even a quick weekend getaway. They want to relax, have fun, and celebrate, but they worry about getting fat and ruining all their progress. So they drive themselves crazy trying to figure out how to mesh "having fun" with "achieving their fitness goals" and eventually just say "screw it" and binge, regret it, and put a massive damper on what was supposed to be a good time.

Screw that.

We're not telling you to binge-eat until you're sick or eat junk for the sake of eating junk. What we *are* saying is, don't worry about ruining your progress during the few times each year you get to relax, take time off work, and enjoy being with your friends and family. Because significant progress isn't made or lost in a day or a week or a month. You don't get fat from your 15 vacation days every year; you get fat based on what you do the other 350 days.

Holidays, birthdays, family celebrations . . . these aren't the time to be worried or meticulous with your nutrition. Relax. Enjoy them. The majority of your year won't be spent partying or celebrating with all-you-can-eat buffets and open bars. The majority of your year is most likely boring, repetitive, and routinized. Except 2020, that was a shit show.

When you're ninety-seven years old, you're not going to think back to your daughter's twelfth birthday and say, "Shucks, I really wish I didn't have that mint chocolate chip ice cream cone." But you will say, "Why was I so uptight? I should have let loose, had more fun, and not let nutrition control every waking moment of my life."

The people who succeed are the ones who understand their progress is not dictated by what they do between Thanksgiving and New Year's Day. Their progress is dictated by what they do between New Year's Day and Thanksgiving.

Make this a personal rule: holidays are holidays. They're not meant for obsessively counting your calories, weighing your food, or bringing your own premade Thanksgiving dinner in Tupperware. Focus on achieving your goals when you're home and in your routine. The few times you're fortunate enough to celebrate holidays and take time off, relax. Have fun. Don't binge for the sake of bingeing. But enjoy yourself and those around you.

Stop Being an Asshole to Yourself

Most people quit for one of two reasons:

1. They think they messed up (we already discussed this and explained why you can't).
2. They think they aren't making progress quickly enough.

Stop. Stop trying to rush the process. Stop being so impatient. Stop expecting rapid results. Stop creating an arbitrary deadline by which you're required to weigh a certain amount. And stop putting unnecessary pressure on yourself to lose weight as quickly as possible.

If it took you 5, 10, 15 years (or more) to get where you are now, you better not believe you're gonna have your dream body in 30, 60, or 90 days. Progress takes time. A lot of time. And if you can justify quitting because you "didn't lose weight quickly enough," you've failed before you've even begun.

Think about it this way. Let's say your friend (we'll call her Pits) "only" lost 2 pounds in the first month of following her new nutrition plan and she was venting about how frustrated she is. Would you tell her she should give up and quit? Would you call Pits a fat mess and ask her why she's even bothering to try anymore?

Of course not. You wouldn't speak to Pits like that, and you shouldn't speak to yourself like that either. It's human nature to be your own harshest critic. But you can't expect to accomplish your goals and love yourself if you constantly speak down to yourself and hold yourself to unrealistic expectations.

Nutrition and exercise are obviously essential for losing weight, getting stronger, building muscle, etc. But the truth is, any physical progress you make without sufficient mental progress is always going to be temporary.

So, if you're serious about achieving your goals, you need to treat yourself like you would treat your best friend. Push yourself to be better. Always strive to improve. But stop being so hard on yourself. Stop speaking so poorly of yourself. Give yourself the greatest opportunity to succeed by holding yourself to your own highest standard while also understanding you're human, there is no rush, and as long as you don't quit you will achieve your goals.

3

Outline Realistic Expectations for Success

You know those memes comparing Expectations vs. Reality?

What you expect you'll do after making New Year's resolutions (work out every day, crush your nutrition, hydrate with water) vs. reality (Netflix, chips and queso, hydrate with wine).

What you expect will earn you points with your partner (flowers, fancy dinner, jewelry) vs. reality (a folded pile of clean laundry, putting the kids to bed, cooking dinner, *and* cleaning the kitchen).

What you expect your fast-food burger to look like based on the commercials (oven-toasted bun, cooked-to-perfection beef patty, freshly picked and vibrantly colored vegetables) vs. reality (soggy bun, lifeless gray patty, and a single shred of seven-month-old brown lettuce).

If we could make a meme of common expectations vs. reality when it comes to fitness goals . . . well, we'd have a lot of them.

Expectation: Lose 1–2 pounds every week for 6 months.

Reality: Week 1—lose 2 pounds; Week 2—lose ½ pound; Week 3—gain 2 pounds; Week 4–Wonder WTF is going on with your scale.

Expectation: Drop 15 pounds and fit into pre-pregnancy jeans in 4 weeks.

Reality: Drop 15 pounds in 4 months, fit into the jeans, still think you need to lose more weight.

Expectation: Eliminate carbohydrates; eat salads and lean protein every meal. Forever.

Reality: Chick-fil-A tastes better than salads. A slice of ice cream cake counts as protein, right? Sushi calories don't count on date night . . .

The problem most people have—at least when it comes to fitness—is they set expectations that are impossible to live up to.

Most people don't realize there is a huge gap between how you *want* weight loss to go and how it actually goes. That's normal. If you're trying to lose weight and you're doing everything right, you'd think you'd, you know . . . lose weight. That's sort of how it works. But not always. And definitely not every day, or even every week. We'll explain.

This chapter will help you set your weight loss expectations so they're based on reality. We'll show you how to track *every* important part of your weight loss journey—most of which people overlook as they obsess over their weight alone. And we'll help you understand these critical truths:

- Your scale weight will never drop in a linear fashion. And that's NORMAL.
- Progress is so much more than the number on your scale. It's the culmination of your weight, strength, habits, and body changes that the scale can't possibly track.
- Mental progress matters, too. Any physical progress you make that is not backed by a strong mindset will be temporary because it's driven by a desire for short-term results. Mental progress can look like sticking to a plan for two weeks straight and still going, when you usually quit after a week. For someone else, mental progress can mean being able to look at the scale without getting emotionally attached to the number.

It would be way easier and much more enjoyable if the scale went down every day. But, unfortunately, that's not how it works. And it's critical for you to understand this because when it doesn't happen as quickly as you want, you need to know it doesn't mean you aren't making progress. As long as you're sticking to your nutrition and training consistently, you *are* making progress. Even if you can't see it every day or every week. You need to learn to be patient and trust the process.

So How Quickly Can You Expect to Lose Weight?

Progress is supposed to be slow. Which sucks, we get it. But just because it's going slower than you want doesn't mean it's not working. Your strength won't increase as quickly as you want. Your weight won't drop as quickly as you want. Your muscles won't become defined as quickly as you want. That's normal, it's part of the process, just keep going.

Many clients trying to lose fat tell us they expect to lose 1–2 pounds every week. And if they don't lose at least that amount on a weekly basis, they give up because they feel like it's not working. First and foremost, that's stupid. Throwing in the towel because progress isn't going as quickly as you'd like is childish. Second, think about it like this: if you lost 2 pounds every week for 6 months, that's 52 pounds. In a year, that's 104 pounds. That's massive. And, candidly, *very few* people can sustain that amount of weight loss each week past the first month or two of dieting. Even a half pound a week is *incredible* progress.

On average, losing 0.5–2 pounds per week is phenomenal progress. The key phrase being "on average." This does *not* mean you will lose 0.5–2 pounds every single week. You won't (especially as you get leaner). This means that, as you analyze your weight loss on a **monthly** basis, you can expect to see an average loss of 1–2 pounds per month (on the low end) and 6–8 pounds per month (on the high end) from the previous month. Keep in mind, if you lost 1–2 pounds, *that is not a bad thing*. It doesn't mean it's not working. Nor does it mean you need to change anything with your workouts or nutrition. Anywhere within the ranges above is *great* progress.

As a general rule, the more body fat you have to lose, the faster you can expect your progress to be. But as you lose body fat, your weight loss will slow down. This does *not* mean you need to change your calorie or nutrition guidelines; it just means you need to stay consistent and stop expecting the scale to go down every day or even every week.

Why Weight Loss Is Never Linear

You can't control your weight on a day-to-day basis, but you can control your consistency, which is why we prefer setting consistency-based goals rather than weight loss goals. Before we dive into that, though, let's dig a little deeper into *why* you can't control your weight on a day-to-day basis, why weight loss is never linear, and equally if not more important: *How do you know you're losing fat if your weight isn't going down?*

Let's set the record straight on daily expectations. We do suggest you track your weight every day *if you can do it without getting attached to the number* (more on that later). But it's not with the sole intention of hoping you've lost weight from day to day. The point is simply to gather data to track your long-term progress. Because that's what this is all about: the long term. Once you've tracked your weight for 30, 60, or 90 days you'll have a comprehensive set of data that clearly shows how much progress you've made and whether you're being as consistent as you need to be. Because when you stay on plan consistently, even if you don't lose weight every day or week, your data points (weigh-ins) will show a clear downward trend. As you track your data on a line graph (which we'll show you in this chapter), the path will look like your walk home after a night of heavy drinking—zigging, zagging, stalling, but eventually reaching your destination.

Now, let's look at why your weight patterns can be so wonky. Why doesn't your weight just keep going down even when your nutrition has been on point and you've been exercising consistently? As it turns out, there are many reasons:

Higher-Than-Normal Sodium Intake

If you eat more salt than usual in a given day, your body will retain water. And you'll likely weigh more the next day because of this. It's no different than if you'd stepped on the scale holding a bottle of water (hint: you'd weigh more). The same is true on the other end of the spectrum: if you eat less salt than usual one day, you may weigh less because you aren't holding on to as much water as you normally do. The fluctuation in either direction has nothing to do with fat gain or loss.

Eating Later or Weighing in Earlier Than Usual

Eating late does not make you gain fat. But if you eat later than you normally would, your weight may spike the next morning simply because you have more food in your stomach. For the same reason, your weight might spike if you weigh yourself earlier in the day than you normally do.

Poop

You can store a surprising amount of weight in your large intestine. You probably don't need us to go deep into the science to understand this one. But if you want to run a little experiment of your own, weigh yourself before and after a solid dookie. You might be surprised at how much you lose.

Weight Lifting

If you've ever weighed yourself the day after a heavy lifting session, you might have noticed your weight spike up. There's a good reason for this, and it has nothing to do with fat gain. Lifting weights damages your muscles (which is a good thing, because from that damage they can repair and grow stronger). But when your muscles get damaged, they soak up water and glycogen (carbohydrates stored in the body) like a sponge, so the scale says you weigh more. This is temporary, 100 percent normal, and not indicative of fat gain. Your body is simply holding on to more water and glycogen. Note: This is especially true for your bigger muscle groups like those in your legs, which is why the weight spike is often more noticeable after lower body workouts.

Stress

Let's be clear: stress isn't inherently a bad thing. You actually need it to survive. You might have heard of cortisol (commonly referred to as the "stress hormone"), but most people don't know cortisol can reduce inflammation, control your blood sugar and blood pressure, and improve your memory formulation.

That said, many people believe stress can make you fat because stress spikes cortisol and cortisol suppresses fat burning. First, they're wrong. And second, that's a massively oversimplified version of how cortisol and your body work. Not to mention, have you ever met someone who loses weight every time they're stressed? This is because some people respond to stress by eating less, while others respond to stress by eating more (hence the term *stress eating*). Stress doesn't make you fat. Eating too many calories on a consistent basis makes you fat. Stress can obviously impact your behavior (eating too much or too little). But stress in and of itself does not dictate whether you gain fat.

It is also worth noting that cortisol can cause your body to hold on to water. And as we've spoken about in this chapter, when your body holds on to water, the scale will spike and say you've gained weight (not fat). Again, that's completely normal, not a bad thing, and it doesn't mean you need to change your diet or exercise. Keep going. Be patient. Eventually your weight will come back down.

Menstrual Cycle

Ladies, we won't go into excruciating detail, but it's important to know your weight *will* spike the week leading up to your period. Some women have a small weight spike of 1–3 pounds, whereas others have a larger weight spike of up to 5–7 pounds. It varies from woman to woman and, interestingly, we've found these weight spikes continue even into menopause. Keep this in mind as you're trying to lose weight, and don't confuse normal weight spikes during your menstrual cycle with fat gain.

Carbohydrates

Eating carbs does not make you fat. When you eat carbs they're stored in your body (mostly your muscles) as glycogen. Now think about what would happen if you slapped a piece of bread on top of spilled water. The bread would soak up the water like a sponge. And that's what happens inside your body. As you eat carbs your body will hold on to water, which can cause the scale to say you've gained weight. But as you know, just because you've gained weight doesn't mean you've gained fat. That said, how much scale weight can you expect to gain from eating carbs?

Let's assume you've been eating fewer carbs than you burn for several days in a row, causing muscle glycogen storage to be low. Then you have a fun night out with friends in which you eat more than usual and polish off a bunch of carbs. Your glycogen stores went from empty to full. Combine that with water retention and you can gain up to 6 pounds of scale weight (not fat) overnight.

If you happen to eat fewer carbs than usual, everything we just said explains why you *lose* weight so quickly, only for the opposite reasons (lower glycogen storage, less water retention, etc.). This is why people rapidly lose weight when they start a low-carb diet like keto. Suddenly eliminating almost all carbohydrates from your diet will cause a rapid weight drop because you're losing water weight (not fat). Unfortunately, this is why so many people who try keto end up gaining all their weight back (and more) as soon as they incorporate carbs back into their diet.

Three Common Weight Loss Patterns

By this point you know your weight will not go down every day or even every week. But even when you understand this, it can still be hard not to get upset on days when your weight spikes up or stays the same, especially when you've been working so damn hard.

Pay attention, because we're going to make dealing with your weight fluctuations a whole lot easier for you. See, over the years coaching thousands of people from all over the world, we've identified the three most common weight loss patterns, and we're going to share each of them with you. Note: These are not necessarily driven by an individual's biology or any specific cause; these are simply common trends we've noticed after seeing thousands of weight loss charts.

Through tracking your weight you'll be able to identify which weight loss pattern your body follows. This way, you can predict and know ahead of time when your weight will spike and when your weight will drop. So, when you want to toss the scale through your bathroom window, you can look at these instead and see what's actually happening and remind yourself that just because your weight went up doesn't mean you're gaining fat.

Harry's Scar

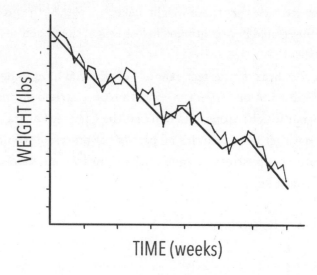

If this is your pattern, you'll usually see quick weight loss within the first 2–4 days of being in a calorie deficit (when you eat fewer calories than you burn on a consistent basis—more on this in Chapter 4). For some people it will be 1 pound. For others it will be more. Either way, you'll lose weight almost immediately after starting your diet. Then after 5–10 days your weight will stall (and maybe spike up to where you began). This is normal. If you stay consistent with your nutrition, your weight will come back down and you'll continue to lose weight. Then, like before, your weight will spike up. This pattern continues until you've lost as much body fat as you want.

Unfortunately, most people don't give it enough time to work because they give up after the first or second weight spike. They don't realize the spikes are normal, so when they see their weight jump up, they have a conniption, tell themselves it's not working, and quit. Whereas if they had just stayed consistent and understood that those weight spikes are part of the process, they would have continued to lose weight slowly and sustainably.

Harry's Scar is a perfect example of why you have to detach your emotions from the scale. Don't get excited on the days your weight drops, and don't let the upswings or stagnant days get you down. It's all part of the process. It could be water, poop, stress . . . any of the things we mentioned earlier. Just keep going.

Downward Staircase

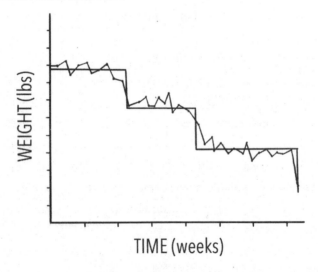

If this is your pattern, you likely won't see much (if any) weight loss within the first 3–7 days of being in a calorie deficit. Remember, this doesn't mean it's not working. This is just another common weight loss pattern. Stay consistent with your nutrition and exercise, and within the first two weeks you'll see a definitive drop on the scale. This doesn't mean it won't spike up again (it probably will), but that's all part of the process. If your weight is following this pattern, you'll see a graph resembling a downward staircase with some random ups and downs along the way. Most people quit when they feel like it's not working because the scale hasn't gone down in "too long" and they think they've hit a "plateau," but don't fall into this mindset. Your weight will continue to drop over time—it just might not happen as quickly as you want. Stay consistent. Don't change anything. Keep going and you will achieve your goal.

The EKG

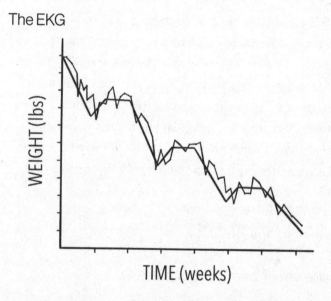

This pattern resembles a combination of the previous two. If your weight loss is following this trend, you'll likely experience a quick drop in weight within the first 2–4 days of being in a calorie deficit. Soon after that, your weight will spike back up, followed by a brief "plateau" (which could last up to a week). Then the pattern starts over as you experience another drop in weight followed by the same cycle until you lose as much body fat as you want. Remember, the spikes and plateaus are normal. They don't mean you're failing or the diet isn't working. It simply means you're human and you need to keep doing exactly what you're doing.

Now that we've explained the three common weight loss patterns, it's important to remember you're not going to lose weight every day or every week. If you lost a pound every week for a year that would be 52 pounds. Not everybody even has 52 pounds to lose. Just track your data and keep going. If you stay 80 percent consistent throughout that time you will notice a downward trend over the long term (30, 60, 90+ days). Even if, during some periods, you don't lose much (or any) weight, it's important to realize that maintaining a lower body weight *is* progress. Every day you maintain a weight that is lower than where you started is another day of progress. And it's another day leading you toward long-term success.

Client Spotlight

Face Your Fears

Susan didn't own a scale for much of her adult life. When she started working with Jordan at age fifty-five, she'd weigh herself only during occasional doctor visits. At home, she tracked progress by her clothing size. Nothing wrong with that. But Susan's reason for avoiding the scale presented an issue.

"Growing up, all I knew was that if the scale went down, it was good. If the scale went up, it was bad," she shared. "If my weight was up, I'd launch into a self-deprecating spiral of, 'What have I done wrong? I must be eating too much. I'm a failure.' When you believe something like that for so long, it's hard to let it go.

"I didn't own a scale because I was petrified of it. I was afraid that if it said a higher number than what I had in my mind, it would confirm I was doing something wrong. And I wouldn't know how to navigate that."

So, when Jordan challenged Susan to track her weight daily, it wasn't because he felt the number was important. It isn't. He wanted to help her develop a healthier relationship with the scale.

"I bought a scale, and I stepped on it every day. I put my daily weight on Instagram just to show people what getting over a fear looks like. Watching my own scale fluctuations was terrifying. I had to learn to drop the idea of 'weigh-in days' and make stepping on the scale part of my routine. It helped me see how what I ate the night before could make me retain water, and how my weight usually drops again the following day. Going through that process on my own has completely changed everything.

"I would be lying if I said that when I see the scale spike, I don't get that little kick in the gut. But the difference now is I don't let my emotions get carried away. I don't freak out about it. I sit with it for a second. Then I move on. I don't care what the number says anymore. The scale doesn't own me. And that's so liberating."

Your Progress Is Not Solely Dictated by the Scale

We know it's easier said than done. But we want you to actively and consciously try to disassociate your emotions from the scale. It has no business dictating how you feel. We're not saying to toss it out altogether (though you can if you want). But try to keep the numbers on the scale separate from your emotions regardless of whether your weight fluctuates up or down. Acknowledge the numbers for what they are—data—and focus on other, more important, markers of progress, like how much strength you've gained, how much better your clothes fit, and how much more confident you feel looking at yourself in the mirror. Because you can be the lightest you've ever been, *feel* like crap, and still not like how you look. And what's the point of that?

Listen, you don't need to weigh yourself. It's not required. So, if the scale makes you miserable, stop weighing yourself for a month and focus on other forms of progress. Whether you're using a scale or not, track as many of these data points as you can each month:

- **How you feel:** Are you more energetic? More confident? Stronger? Do you have less joint pain? Are you less out of breath when you walk up the stairs? These are tremendous markers of progress that are equally (if not more) important than the scale.

- **Belt size:** Can you use a tighter belt notch? Good, you're losing fat (even if the scale hasn't gone down).
- **Measurements:** Are your measurements going down? Perfect, decreasing waist and hip measurements are phenomenal indicators of fat loss.
- **Pictures:** Do you see more definition in your pictures? Notice spots where fat is clearly going down and you're getting more defined? You're on the right track. Sometimes the scale barely moves, but you'll notice a huge difference in your pictures over time.
- **Clothing size:** Are your pants looser? Can you fit into something you haven't been able to wear in a long time? It doesn't matter what the scale says because you're clearly making progress.

By all means, use the scale as a tool. But remember the scale means nothing compared to how you look and feel. The scale is not always indicative of fat loss (or gain). And if you mainly focus on trying to move the scale, you'll end up looking for short-term fixes instead of long-term solutions.

Client Spotlight

Get Excited about the Right Things

Kim describes herself as a formerly-obese-person-turned-powerlifter. She started working with Jordan four years ago because she wanted help getting stronger. What she didn't realize she needed, though, was to develop a better relationship with food and the scale.

"Part of our work together included having me send Jordan my weight every day. And he never responded the way I thought he would," Kim remembers. "I'm not even talking about what he said—but what he didn't say. On days my weight went down, he was totally neutral. To the point where I wondered whether he was even reading my emails. But he was. And those reactions taught me one of the biggest lessons about weight loss: If we get too excited about the days when the scale is down, what does that say about the days when it's up? That we should be equally upset? Absolutely not.

"That helped me develop a very neutral relationship with the scale; to see it as an individual data point, and to not put stock in any one data point. I stopped comparing my weight today with my weight yesterday, or even my weight last week. Instead, I looked at big chunks of time—a month, six weeks, eight weeks. And I learned to stop letting what the scale said dictate my actions. So, if the scale went up, it didn't mean I screwed up or had to eat less that day. It just meant the scale was up. That's it."

Now Kim tracks progress through measurements (waist, butt, and thighs) and pictures. "It is so incredible to notice the difference in your pictures, because once you're pretty lean, the scale is not going to change all that much. What changes is how you look.

"I'm up 10 pounds from when I started, but I'm in the best shape of my life. I have more muscle. I have more definition. I still wear the same size pants even though my weight is up. As a forty-eight-year-old mom of three, I bought a bikini for the first time in my adult life. The last time I'd worn a bikini I was nineteen years old and felt self-conscious the whole time. I never put one on again until last year."

The Most Overlooked and Underrated Form of Progress

Your weight, measurements, pictures, and clothing size are great ways to measure your progress. But they aren't the only way. And before we end this chapter, it's critical for you to recognize the most overlooked and underrated form of progress: mental progress. Especially because mental progress looks different for everyone.

Some people struggle with self-control. They want to lose fat but have trouble saying "no." Often, they'll justify eating inordinate amounts of junk food by saying they're "flexible dieting." But flexible dieting doesn't mean "eat junk, lose fat." It means "don't feel guilty for having a treat—but the majority of your diet should still be whole, minimally processed foods that help you look and feel your best." For them, progress might look like saying "no" to the doughnut so they can stay on track.

Other people struggle with food anxiety. They get anxious at the thought of going out to eat because they don't want to "ruin their progress." They feel bad for having a slice of cake at their own birthday party. Logically, they know it sounds silly and they often give their friends/family/clients amazing nutrition advice that promotes a more flexible approach . . . but they struggle with it themselves. For them, progress might look like saying "yes" to the doughnut without getting anxious or feeling like a failure.

Progress is not only measured in weight loss or measurements or other quantifiable data. Progress is also measured in mental, emotional, and behavioral changes. If you don't improve your mindset first, any physical changes or improvements are going to be short-lived. Because sustainable results happen only with a sustainable mindset.

Remember, what you weigh today, or next week, or next month, doesn't matter. In twenty years, you won't care what you weighed this morning. You will care about your relationship with food. Focus on building sustainable habits long term. Because once you can do that, you've already won.

A Random Story: How Gary Vee Gained Five Pounds in Three Hours

This is a true story. Every word. And anytime someone gets worried because their weight spiked up a few pounds, this is what we tell them.

It starts with Gary Vaynerchuk (who wrote the foreword for this book), one of the world's most successful and highly sought-after entrepreneurs. Mike coached Gary for two years, followed by Jordan, who coached him for the next three years. It was a life-changing opportunity to coach Gary and, frankly, we were both petrified when we initially took the job. We both looked up to Gary immensely, followed him on social media, and read all of his books. We couldn't believe he wanted each of us to coach him. It was an intense job—traveling with him all over the world, coaching him seven days a week, no vacations or weekends off—but we jumped at the chance to coach him.

When Mike's two years with Gary were up, Jordan moved all the way from Israel to NYC to take over as Gary's coach and Mike stayed on for one extra month to oversee the transition. Jordan's first few days coaching Gary took place on a sunny, beautiful holiday weekend in late May of 2016 at Gary's summer home. Jordan still couldn't believe he got the job and was a nervous wreck every time he interacted with Gary (which Mike thought was hysterical).

Now, it's worth mentioning, one of the major reasons Gary hired us was so he could have, in his words, "a nutritional babysitter." He said he had very little self-control around food and, since he had the money, he wanted to pay a coach to watch his every bite. Through working with him we taught him the principles outlined in this book, and he no longer needs that level of coaching, but early on we paid *very* close attention to his diet.

Back to Jordan's first weekend on the job. Gary weighed in at 168 pounds that Saturday before he headed to a New York Mets game in the city. He had box seats and told Jordan to text him regularly to make sure he wasn't overdoing it with all the food they had in the suite. Jordan agreed, told him to enjoy himself, focus on protein, and reminded him they would get right back on track the next day. Halfway through the second inning, Jordan nervously sent his first text.

How you doing, Gary?

No response.

Heading into the fourth inning, Jordan sent his second text, getting increasingly anxious that he was annoying Gary.

Sorry to bother you, Gary, just seeing how you're doing with food?

No response.

By this point, Jordan was ready to call it quits. He didn't want to piss Gary off and risk losing his job. He told Mike that Gary still hadn't replied after two texts, to which Mike said, "Text him again." You see, Mike had two years of experience in situations like this, and he knew Gary both appreciated and responded well to persistence.

I'm really sorry, Gary, but is everything okay at the game?

Again, no response.

Coming up to the seventh inning Mike had had enough. "Call him," he told Jordan.

Jordan's head snapped up and he made eye contact with Mike. "Are you serious?" he asked.

"Yes," Mike said, "call him right now."

Heart beating out of his chest, nervous that he was interrupting an important business meeting and was about to get fired, Jordan called Gary.

Call ignored. Not just missed. Gary ignored the call and sent it straight to voicemail.

"Call him again," Mike said immediately.

Jordan couldn't take the pressure anymore. "You call him," he snapped back.

Without hesitation, Mike called Gary.

Again, straight to voicemail.

"Should we leave a message?" Jordan asked.

There was a long, drawn-out pause.

"No . . . he's gone," Mike said with a sigh.

The next day, we woke up to someone knocking quickly and loudly on our bedroom door. It was Gary. We shot out of bed, opened the door, and anxiously asked him how it went at the game last night.

Gary barely made eye contact with us. Shuffling his feet like a young child who knew he'd done something he wasn't supposed to, Gary looked up with a furrowed brow and quietly said "It was bad."

Jordan couldn't believe it. This whole time he thought Gary was going to be pissed that he kept calling him during the game when, in reality, Gary was disappointed in himself.

"What do you mean?" Jordan asked.

Gary paused. "It was *really* bad," he said.

"I'm sure it wasn't that bad," Jordan replied. "And, regardless, we're gonna get right back on track today. One bad day doesn't make or break your progress."

Gary shook his head. "You don't understand, Jord. I ate *a lot*."

"Wings?" Mike asked, knowing how much Gary loved wings.

"No," Gary replied, still looking at the ground and shuffling his feet.

"Burgers and fries?" Jordan asked.

"No," Gary said again.

"Wine?" asked Mike.

"No."

"So what'd you have?" asked Jordan.

Gary paused, looking overwhelmingly ashamed of himself. As though he'd made a huge, irreversible mistake.

"Beans," he muttered.

"Beans?" Jordan asked.

"Beans," Gary repeated.

"Beans?" Mike asked again.

"Beans," Gary said one more time. "A lot of beans."

"Beans aren't bad," Jordan told him.

"No," Gary interrupted. "You don't understand. I ate *a lot* of beans."

"How many beans did you eat?" Mike asked.

Gary paused again.

"It started with a plate," he said. "You know those BBQ baked beans I like a lot? I had a whole plate thinking that would be plenty. Then I had a second plate. And before I knew it, I ate the entire tray." Gary held out his arms to show the size of a massive tray of beans.

"You ate the whole tray of beans?" Jordan asked.

"Like, the entire thing?" Mike added on.

"The entire thing," Gary said.

When he stepped on the scale after his beans confession, he weighed in at 173 pounds, 5 pounds heavier than the previous day. Within three days he was back down to 168 pounds. He didn't starve himself. He didn't do hours of extra cardio. He just got right back on track and focused on hitting his calories and emphasizing protein at every meal.

We shared this story because we know it can be frustrating when the scale spikes up. We know it can be scary when you enjoy yourself on one random occasion and see the scale soar upwards of 5 pounds in a day. That being said, you can't let it get to you. And you can't let it convince you that you've lost all your progress. Because you haven't. The scale is not the be-all and end-all, and it doesn't tell you the whole story. Regardless of what the scale says, just keep going. No matter what.

Part II
Eat It!

4

Flexible Dieting

Keto and low-carb fanatics will say the reason you lose fat following their diet is because carbs make you fat, but in reality you've just eliminated an entire macronutrient, so you're eating fewer calories. Low-fat zealots will say the reason you lose fat using their approach is because fat makes you fat, but, again, in reality you've drastically reduced an entire macronutrient so you're eating fewer calories. Intermittent fasting extremists will say the reason you lose fat with their protocol is because it optimizes your fat loss hormones, but in reality you've just reduced how much time you spend eating so you're eating fewer calories. The paleo cult will say the reason you lose fat is because you're eating like our ancestors, but in reality you're just focusing on low-calorie, nutrient-dense foods so you're eating fewer calories.

The only way to lose fat is to eat fewer calories. And, more specifically, to eat in a calorie deficit.

We'll tell you exactly how many calories you need to be eating to lose fat later on (Chapter 9), but for now the most important things for you to understand are:

- If you eat in a calorie surplus, you'll gain weight.
- If you eat in a calorie deficit, you'll lose weight.
- If you eat at your maintenance calorie intake, you'll stay roughly the same.

Does this mean you can lose fat while eating any foods you want? Yes, that's exactly what it means (and it's one of the reasons we named this book *Eat It!*; because you can eat any food you want while losing fat). Does that mean you should only eat Twinkies and Pop-Tarts? Of course not. Just because you can lose fat while eating your favorite foods doesn't mean it's healthy to *only* eat your favorite foods while losing fat. We'll talk more about this later, but for now it's important to understand that the only way to lose fat is to be in a calorie deficit. As long as you do that, you can (and should) include your favorite foods in moderation to make the process more enjoyable and sustainable.

What Is Flexible Dieting?

The fitness industry runs on a pendulum of extremes. As a result, flexible dieting has been misconstrued from what began as a way to enjoy your favorite foods in moderation into a justification to eat as much pizza, candy, and processed foods as possible, as long as it fits within your calories.

Let us be abundantly clear: flexible dieting done properly is not about eating as many sweets and treats as possible within your calorie range. Flexible dieting is being able to include your favorite foods within your diet without feeling guilty, worried, or anxious that you're doing something wrong or ruining your progress.

Flexible dieting is being able to enjoy a few slices of pizza at your daughter's birthday party without feeling like you should starve yourself the rest of the week to "make up for the damage." Flexible dieting is being able to have some beers and hot wings with your buddies without feeling obligated to punish yourself with two hours of fasted cardio the next morning. Flexible dieting is eating an overall healthy, nutrient-dense diet filled with lots of fruits, vegetables, lean proteins, healthy fats, and water while including your favorite foods in moderation throughout the week. And the first step to a healthier diet starts with understanding calories.

Good Calories vs. Bad Calories

Many people think there are "good" calories and "bad" calories. Heck, there are entire books written on which foods you are allowed to eat and which you aren't. All calories are created equal. While many people get upset when we say this, it's the truth. Keep in mind, we're not saying all foods affect the body equally. They don't. And anyone who says they do is an asshat. We are saying, however, that a calorie is always a calorie regardless of where it comes from, and we're going to tell you why.

First and foremost, what is a calorie? By definition, a calorie is a unit of energy. Specifically, a unit of energy that tells us how much energy is in a given food. That's it. It doesn't tell us about the micronutrient composition of the food, it doesn't tell us how much fat or sugar or protein or carbohydrates are in the food, it doesn't tell us how much fiber the food has, and it doesn't tell us how the food is going to make us feel.

Think of it this way. A mile is a unit of length. Specifically, a unit of length that tells us how long a given distance is. It doesn't matter if the mile is on pavement, in the forest, on sand, going uphill or downhill . . . a mile is always a mile. The composition of each mile drastically changes and can affect how long it would take you to run it. For example, it would likely take longer for you to run a mile on sand than it would to run a mile on pavement. But it doesn't change the fact that you're still running a mile.

The same goes for calories: 100 calories from an apple are the same as 100 calories from a doughnut. The apple is obviously more nutrient dense, would fill you up more, and will likely make you feel better. Which is why the apple is traditionally seen as the "healthier" choice. But that doesn't change the fact that 100 apple calories are the same as 100 doughnut calories no matter what.

So Doughnuts Are the Same As Apples?

No. Of course not, dummy. The apple has infinitely more vitamins and minerals. The apple is significantly more nutrient dense. The apple has more fiber. And the apple is, from a physiological perspective, a better choice the majority of the time.

That being said, weight loss and health are not purely physiological. If they were, you wouldn't be reading this book. Everyone would just "eat less and move more" and no one would struggle with their weight. And, frankly, we wouldn't have a job. But that's not how this works.

Weight loss and health are equal parts physiological and psychological. And research consistently shows that flexible dieters (those who can include their favorite foods in moderation on a regular basis) are more successful at maintaining a healthier body weight than rigid dieters (those who think they need to be ruthlessly strict for their entire life). Which makes sense, because you can sustain a flexible diet forever, whereas you can only sustain a rigid diet for so long before you quit.

Our goal isn't to get you to lose weight as quickly as possible, only for you to regain it (and more). Our goal is to help you lose any unwanted body fat in a way that allows you to enjoy your favorite foods and maintain your weight loss for the rest of your life.

We're not telling you to eat doughnuts instead of apples. We're telling you to, most of the time, choose the food that is going to help you look and feel your best. And, some of the time, choose the food that gives you an orgasm in your mouth. And remember, if the methods are unsustainable, the results are unsustainable.

Having said all of that, our genius editor, Rebecca, told us we need better transitions. So let's dive into macronutrients.

Macros, Micros, and Mike's Macros

First and foremost, if you haven't downloaded Mike's Macros, Mike's app for calorie and macro tracking, do that right now. Seriously. It's in the App Store. It's free. There are no ads. And it's far and away the best calorie/macro tracking app currently available. So go download it real quick and then keep reading.

Downloading . . .

Now that you've downloaded the app, let's discuss what macros are, why they're important, and how you're going to use them to your advantage.

Macro is short for macronutrient, which is a type of food required in large amounts in the diet (different from *micronutrients*, which are required in small amounts). There are three main macronutrients: protein, carbohydrates, and fat. Alcohol is, technically, the fourth macronutrient, but as long as you aren't slamming shots for breakfast and treating alcohol like a major food group, we don't need to bore you with the science.

That said, we're going to throw some numbers at you. Bear with us and don't skip ahead because this is critical for you to understand. And, we promise, we'll make it clear, easy to grasp, and as quick as possible.

- Protein has 4 calories per gram
- Carbohydrates have 4 calories per gram
- Fat has 9 calories per gram
- And, if you're curious, alcohol has 7 calories per gram

All food has at least one of these macronutrients. And many foods contain two or sometimes three. Eggs, for example, are a combination of both protein and fat. Chicken breast is almost purely protein. And rice is nearly all carbohydrates. Suffice to say all foods include at least one macronutrient, and each macronutrient contains a certain number of calories.

All Calories Are Created Equal; All Macronutrients Are Not

You already know why all calories are created equal. But all macronutrients are not, and in this section we're going to explain the unique benefits each macronutrient supplies to your body and why it's better to include them all rather than eliminate any of them altogether.

Also worth noting, in the Appendix you'll find our Macros Cheat Sheet (page 207) with some examples of our favorite protein, carbohydrate, and fat sources.

Protein

If you take only one thing from this section, let it be this: protein is the "king" macronutrient, and emphasizing it within your diet will help you lose fat, build muscle, increase your strength, and stay full while eating fewer calories. Strategically increasing your protein intake is one of the simplest, easiest, and most effective ways to achieve your goals.

Here are a few reasons why protein is so beneficial:

1. **Protein is the only macronutrient that can help build or maintain muscle.** This is important because if you're in a calorie deficit *and* you're not getting enough protein, you will lose muscle as your body uses it for other processes. Muscle is more metabolically active than any other tissue in your body. So, the more muscle you have, the faster your metabolism is going to be, and the more calories you'll burn even when you're just sitting still (more on all this in Chapter 5). Maintaining your muscle mass will also help keep your energy and strength up—both keys to generally feeling well.

2. **Protein tends to be the most filling macronutrient, so it keeps you full for fewer calories.** One of the main reasons people give up and fail with their diets is because they constantly feel hungry and deprived. Which makes sense because they're usually doing something stupid like a juice fast or a detox cleanse. That said, even if you're eating intelligently with nutrient-dense foods, it can be difficult to stay consistent with your diet if you're always hungry. This is where protein reigns king. Research consistently shows protein is the most filling of all macronutrients by a long shot.

3. **Protein has the highest thermic effect of food (TEF).** TEF is a component of your metabolism that measures how much energy your body uses to digest, absorb, and dispose of all of the nutrients it's taking in. Protein has the highest TEF compared to other macronutrients, which means it gets your body to burn the most calories just by processing what you eat. More on TEF in Chapter 5.

We'll talk more about how much protein you should eat later on, but for now we want you to emphasize protein at every meal. As long as you do that, you're going to be feeling fuller, giving your body the nutrients it needs to build muscle, and increasing your metabolism.

Carbohydrates

First and foremost, carbohydrates do not make you fat. If you follow anyone who tells you otherwise, unfollow them immediately. If any of your friends or family members tell you carbohydrates make you fat, kindly ask them why the Japanese eat white rice daily and are among the healthiest populations in the world. You can also ask them why the results of literally every well-performed study have shown calories—not carbohydrates—dictate fat gain or loss.[*] Then you can smile at them and wait while they stumble over their words and fail to produce a coherent response.

Carbohydrates are incredibly helpful to and important for your body, especially when it comes to your strength and performance. If you're the least bit interested in getting stronger, building muscle, getting more defined, and being more athletic, carbohydrates are the fuel source that will help you achieve those goals. They also massively enhance your mood and, let's be honest, taste amazing.

It's important to keep in mind we're not telling you to stuff

[*] K. D. Hall and J. Guo, "Obesity Energetics: Body Weight Regulation and the Effects of Diet Composition," *Gastroenterology*, U.S. National Library of Medicine, https://pubmed.ncbi.nlm.nih.gov/28193517/. Accessed November 4, 2021.

your face full of carbohydrates every chance you get. And, realistically, most people struggling with their weight would do well to increase their protein intake and decrease their carb and fat intake. That said, it's critical for you to understand carbohydrates are not inherently bad for you, they do not inherently make you fat, and you should eat them on a regular basis to optimize your health and performance and stay more consistent with your diet.

Fat

Dietary fat (the fat in your food) and body fat (the fat in your body, duh) are not the same thing. And eating fat doesn't inherently make you fat. Eating too many calories does. Dietary fat is overwhelmingly important for your health and well-being and plays a massive role in regulating your hormonal health. So any diet that tells you to eliminate fat is based on, literally, zero credible scientific evidence. And it will do far more harm than good, especially considering you need dietary fat in order to survive. Seriously. If you don't eat fat, you will die. That's not hyperbole. Onward.

Health vs. Fat Loss

You already know the only way to lose fat is to be in a calorie deficit. And you also know that you can enjoy your favorite foods while in a calorie deficit and continue to lose body fat. But it's important to understand that just because you can lose weight eating junk food does not mean it's healthy to eat only junk food, *even if you're losing weight*.

Health and fat loss are not one and the same. They're certainly intertwined (think of them overlapping in a Venn diagram), but just because you can lose weight eating candy and pizza and burgers and fries doesn't make it healthy. A healthy diet mostly (not solely) consists of whole, minimally processed, nutrient-dense foods. Lots of water, fruits, vegetables, lean proteins, whole grains, beans, lentils, and high-quality fats.

We wrote this book to help you develop a healthier relationship with food so you can enjoy your favorite foods without any guilt or shame while continuing to lose fat. But this book would be severely misleading if we didn't highlight the importance of making sure the majority of your diet is made up of foods that not only help you lose weight but are also minimally processed, high in fiber, and rich in vitamins and minerals, and contribute to bettering your overall health. Again, we have included samples of these foods for your reference in our Macros Cheat Sheet in the Appendix.

From Beginner to Advanced: Learning How to Diet

As much as we talk about calorie counting, we believe the ultimate form of "diet mastery" is being able to maintain a healthy body weight without meticulously tracking each and every bite of food.

The reason we go into so much detail about calorie counting, though, is because using a more advanced, intuitive approach is a skill. It takes a lot of time, effort, patience, and consistency to develop. And just as you don't first learn how to ride a bike by entering into a BMX competition, you don't learn how to lose body fat and keep it off by jumping into the most advanced dieting progression. That's why when you start losing weight (no matter how many times you've tried in the past), you need to go through the mastery process:

First, gain the knowledge: Understand calories and macros, find the best meal frequency for you (Chapter 8), and understand a realistic rate of progression (Chapter 3).

Second, develop the skills: Master calorie counting, practice meal planning, and learn to recognize your trigger foods (the foods you struggle to stop eating once you start).

Third, learn the "tricks of the trade" to make dieting easier: Understand how to make progress without counting calories and learn what to eat so you can stay full while in a calorie deficit (Chapter 8).

Remember, flexible dieting is a skill. Using an intuitive approach is only possible once you've taken the time to learn what works best for you. This isn't something you'll master in a day or a week or a month. In our experience it can take anywhere from one to five years of consistent practice. You don't need to count calories forever (unless you want to). But if you'd like to get to a point where you don't have to track your calories, you first need to master the skills that will help you get there.

Client Spotlight

To Track, or Not to Track?

"I trained with Mike for eight weeks, and during that time, I tracked every bite I ate in the Mike's Macros app. After dedicating those eight weeks to superdiligent tracking, it became really easy to understand what I should eat, and how much of it, to stay in a calorie deficit. Building that knowledge made this sustainable. I don't want to track every single thing I eat for the rest of my life."

—*Danny*

"Before working with Mike, I knew the general principles of eating healthy, but I had never thought about how many calories I'd need to eat if I want to lose weight. Tracking was helpful because it really helps you build that skill. And after you've done it long enough, you don't have to be so detail-oriented. You just know what four ounces of chicken looks like, or that if you cook with a certain amount of oil, you need to keep it in mind toward your calories. But I still track my calories every day. I've been doing it for six years. I like that precision. It's just how I'm wired."

—*Chris*

The Fat Loss Food Pyramid

The original food pyramid wasn't the worst nutrition advice we've ever seen. But it wasn't the best thing to happen to our societal waistline, mainly because of the overemphasis on bread, grains, and cereal and a lack of emphasis on protein.

We've always loved the idea of a food pyramid, though. A clear hierarchy of nutritional importance so you know which food groups to prioritize on a daily basis. So we made our own. It's not complicated or fancy. But it works very well. And if you stick to the guidelines, you will be able to lose fat (and keep it off) while enjoying your favorite foods.

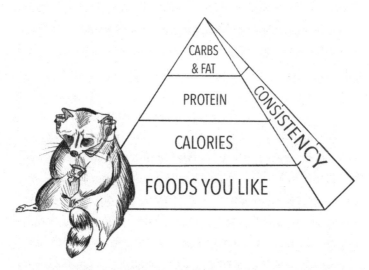

You'll notice consistency scales the entire length of the Fat Loss Food Pyramid. That's because without consistency, the whole operation falls apart. If you want to get and stay lean (no yo-yo dieting), you need to be consistent. Not perfect. But consistent. Because sustainable progress comes from dietary flexibility, not rigidity. There will be times when you're stressed, or super busy, or just want to eat more than your calorie allotment for the day. And that's okay. It's not realistic to expect yourself to hit your calories every single day. So go for the classic 80/20 rule. Aim to hit your calories 80 percent of the time. The other 20 percent, give yourself wiggle room. Have some pizza and *enjoy it*. You can even eat your favorite foods and still stay within your calorie goals.

With consistency as king, each layer of the pyramid represents your priorities, in order of importance, from bottom to top. **Foods you like** are the foundation and biggest priority. And they go hand in hand with consistency because if you don't like what you're eating, you won't stick to the plan. To be clear, "foods you like" should be *mostly nutrient-dense foods that you enjoy eating*. But there is also room to include anything else you want. **Calories** are next, because, you know, that whole calorie deficit thing. From there, we focus on your macronutrients: **protein**, **carbs**, and **fat**. Let's take a closer look at each layer.

Priority 1: Foods You Like

We know: after all the fuss we made about calories being the only thing that matters for fat loss, how can we say foods you like are the top priority? We get tons of resistance on

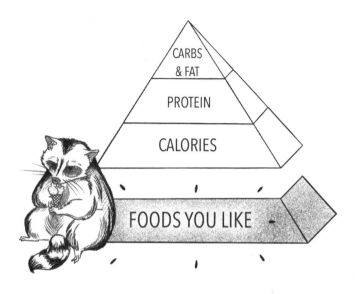

this point. It may seem counterintuitive, but eating foods you like is critical. Here's why:

The 80/20 rule gives you flexibility. But staying on track 80 percent of the time will still be hard. We don't care how "perfect" your diet looks on paper. If you don't like the foods you're eating, you're eventually going to quit. We don't want you to hit your calorie target at the expense of your joy and sanity. You're more likely to stick with this, and be happy, if you like what you're eating every day. This means something very important: **Make sure you enjoy the nutrient-dense foods that make up most of your diet.**

The rest of the pyramid offers guidelines on choosing nutrient-dense foods. But we never tell you exactly what to eat. It is your choice because you need to like what you're eating. Sure, cottage cheese is low-calorie and high-protein, but if the look and smell of it makes you nauseous, don't eat it. Try Greek yogurt instead. Tofu grosses you out? Cool, us, too. Grill up some salmon instead. Many people think eating "healthy" sucks because they think they're only allowed to eat celery and drink lemon water. That's nonsense. And the sooner you realize healthy eating doesn't equate to eating like a rabbit, the sooner you'll be able to achieve and sustain your goals.

Priority 2: Calories

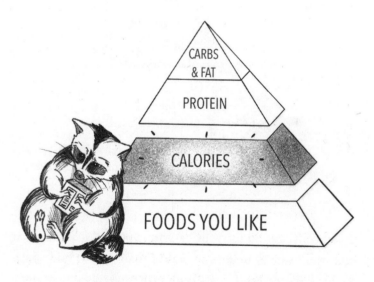

You already know the only way to lose fat is to be in a calorie deficit. It doesn't matter how "clean" or "healthy" you eat, if you aren't in a calorie deficit, you won't lose fat. That's why once you've got "consistency" and "foods you like" nailed down, you need to get your calories in check. We'll tell you exactly how many calories you need to eat to lose fat later on (Chapter 9), but for now suffice to say hitting your calories on a daily basis is your nutritional priority (far more than hitting your carbs, fat, and even protein).

Priority 3: Protein

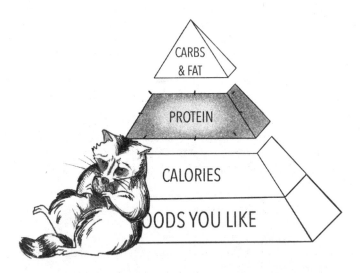

If you consistently hit your calories, you will lose fat. That said, you want to make sure you're fueling your body optimally and, specifically, eating enough protein.

People often think they only need to worry about protein only if they're lifting weights, but that couldn't be farther from the truth. If you want to lose fat as comfortably and sustainably as possible, protein will help you do exactly that. No, it won't magically make you bulky. No, it won't make you look like a bodybuilder. It will help keep you full. It will increase your metabolism. And it will help you get stronger and more defined and recover from workouts.

Priority 4: Carbs and Fat

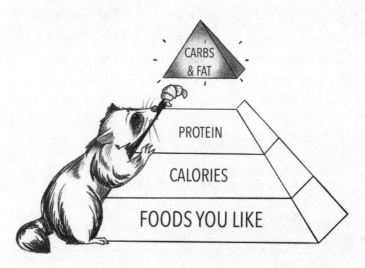

By the end of this book you'll be whispering "calorie deficit" in your sleep. You may even name your first-born child Calorie Deficit. Because by the end of this book you'll fully understand the *only* way to lose fat is to be in a calorie deficit regardless of how many carbs and how much fat you're eating. That's why carbs and fats are the top of the Fat Loss Food Pyramid—because it doesn't matter how many carbs and how much fat you eat as long as your calories are in check. And as long as you do that, you will lose fat.

And if you're about to have a conniption, wondering why it doesn't matter how many carbs and how much fat you eat, remember that it's impossible to gain fat if you're in a calorie deficit. And as long as your calories are in check, you can fit as many carbs and as much fat as you want *within your calorie guidelines* and still lose fat. We're not saying, "Eat as many carbs and as much fat as humanly possible." We're saying, "Eat as many carbs and as much fat as you want within your calorie guidelines."

Client Spotlight

Food Doesn't Have Moral Value

"I spent a lifetime yo-yo dieting. When I finally grasped the concept that I need to stay in a calorie deficit to lose weight, I still had that 'cheat day' mentality strongly embedded in my mind since I'd entered the fitness world through the bodybuilding side of things. I would always tell myself, 'If I was good enough, I could cheat and have the pizza,' but I *had to be good enough.*

"Jordan changed all that for me. He taught me that food doesn't have moral value. That you don't need to earn your pizza by enduring salad all week long, and by the way, your salad should taste good. It shouldn't be some dry little salad that you hate so you can then earn your pizza on cheat day."

—*Kim*

How Many Meals Should You Eat per Day?

You might have heard some "experts" say you need to eat six small meals a day to "stoke your metabolic fire." You might have heard other "experts" say breakfast is the biggest and most important meal of the day, whereas dinner should be the smallest. You've probably heard other "experts" say you should never eat after 6:00 p.m. or 8:00 p.m. or 9:32 p.m. (depending on which charlatan's Instagram page you landed on). And, unfortunately, you've likely heard other "experts" say you should only eat one giant meal per day because that's what our ancestors did when they were cavemen. So what the heck are you supposed to actually do?

Fortunately, the truth is far simpler than many make it out to be: you can eat however many meals you like, at whatever time of day you like, as long as your total daily calories are in check. It doesn't matter if you prefer three square meals each day, six small meals each day, or twenty-one thimble-sized meals each day; if your total calorie intake is in line with your goals, your results will be the same.

From a practical standpoint, it probably doesn't make sense to eat twenty-one thimble-sized meals. In fact, please don't do that. That's dumb. But, for what it's worth, research examining the effect of meal frequency on metabolism studied everything from one meal a day all the way up to six meals a day, and it found no difference in the net metabolic effect as long as daily calories were equivalent.

Having said all of that, once you've established which

meal frequency works best for you and your individual preferences, it is helpful to do your best to stick to that schedule as closely as possible. Reason being, your body's hunger hormones (leptin, ghrelin, peptide YY, etc.) can be "trained" so you get hungry at similar times each day as long as you stick to a consistent eating schedule. This can be incredibly helpful, especially if you're trying to lose weight, so you can know ahead of time when you'll be hungry and can prepare for it.

For example, if you regularly eat lunch around 1:00 p.m., you'll notice yourself getting hungry around 1:00 p.m. every day. Keep in mind, this "training process" can take up to 2–4 weeks of consistency, so don't expect your body to adapt to this new schedule within 7 minutes of starting your new diet. Give it a chance, be consistent, and over the course of your first month you'll notice your hunger kicking in right on schedule. Just make sure to keep your eating schedule similar on the weekends as well.

If you're wondering what the best meal frequency is . . . stop. Stop looking for "the best." Everyone wants "the best" diet, "the best" workout, "the best" meal plan, blah blah blah. There is no "best." Because the only true "best" meal frequency (and plan, overall) is the one you can stick to consistently over the long haul. So take 15 minutes out of your day to sit down, look at your daily schedule, and plan a meal frequency you think will work best for you. Give it a fair shot (at least 30 days), and if it works, great, stick with it. If it doesn't, cool, try a new one. Again, the most important thing is hitting your calories on a consistent basis. Whichever meal frequency allows you to do that as easily as possible is the best one for you.

Everything you've learned throughout this chapter will help you become a successful flexible dieter. But no matter how many tricks or strategies we give you, the most important thing for you to understand and internalize is that consistency is far more important than perfection. This isn't an all-or-nothing game. And the sooner you start fitting nutrition into your life (rather than trying to fit life into your nutrition), the sooner you will be able to achieve your goals while building a healthy relationship with food.

5

WTF Is Metabolism?

Most people who are obsessed with the idea of "speeding up their metabolism" don't know what their metabolism actually is. And nearly all the people selling you "metabolism-boosting" pills, powders, drinks, and body wraps are just trying to steal your hard-earned money (and most of them don't even know how to spell *metabolism*).

Ask any person who wants to "boost their metabolism" to define the word. Most will tell you something like, "I'm not exactly sure, but I do know mine is way slower than it should be." And they'll likely follow it with a story about their friend who can eat Taco Bell chalupas every day and still have a perfectly flat stomach or a six-pack year-round because their metabolism is so fast. They hate that friend because they feel like that person can eat whatever they want without worrying about getting fat while they get a quadruple chin from so much as looking at a Krispy Kreme doughnut.

There are many misconceptions around what metabolism is, how it works, and how we can control it. The amount of misinformation on this topic can drive anyone to doubt themselves and worry about whether their body will ever let them lose weight and keep it off forever. Take a breather. Relax. Let's chill out with the metabolism hysteria. Because most of the things people worry about (broken metabolism, age, gender, hormonal imbalance, etc.) are exaggerated at best and completely inaccurate at worst. And as they fixate their attention on the minutiae, they overlook the behaviors that are actually derailing their progress. Keep in mind, hormonal imbalances and metabolic disorders do exist; they are very real and can make weight loss harder. That said, most people who *think* they have a hormonal imbalance or metabolic disorder haven't actually seen a doctor to get tested. So, if you think you have one of these issues, ask your doctor to take your blood work so you can know definitively whether this is something you need to address.

Okay. Let's take a step back.

Metabolism. Yours isn't "broken," so unfollow the twenty-two-year-old Instagram influencer who keeps telling you it is, and pay attention to what we're saying. Your metabolism is the sum of the chemical processes going on in your body to keep you alive. Literally everything your body does: cell growth and repair, building bones, making red blood cells, digestion, muscle growth, blinking, breathing . . . they all contribute to your metabolism.

We consulted with our friend and trusted authority on the topic, Dr. Spencer Nadolsky, to help zero in on the parts of metabolism that are essential to understand for fat loss. Dr. Nadolsky is a board-certified physician specializing in obesity medicine. He works with clients worldwide to help them use exercise and nutrition to get lean and reverse their medical issues. Here's what we've learned.

Metabolic Rate

Your metabolic rate is the rate at which you burn energy (i.e., calories). It's broken into two components: **basal metabolic rate (BMR)** and **resting metabolic rate (RMR)**. Many people use these terms interchangeably, but they're not the same thing.

Your basal metabolic rate (BMR) measures the calories your body needs to survive at a bare minimum—basically, just keeping your organs functioning while you sleep. It's not a practical measurement for everyday life since you probably do more than . . . well, nothing.

Your resting metabolic rate (RMR) measures the energy your body needs to survive in normal everyday activities. Right now, you're probably sitting down and relaxing, but you're using your muscles to hold yourself upright. If you're lying down, you're holding this book. You're using your eyes to read and your brain to think and comprehend these words. Your digestive system is processing your last meal. All those functions are bundled into your RMR.

If you ever want to calculate your metabolic rate, your RMR is the more relevant measurement since it includes all of your everyday bodily functions. And it's what we're referring to here when we talk about your metabolic rate.

In addition to RMR, these are the three other components of your metabolic rate:

- **Thermic effect of activity (TEA):** how many calories your body burns from planned exercise (cardio, weight lifting, sports, etc.).
- **Non-exercise activity thermogenesis (NEAT):** how many calories your body burns from any and all movement that isn't planned exercise (including things like fidgeting, foot tapping, raking leaves, washing the dishes, etc.).
- **Thermic effect of food (TEF):** how many calories your body burns from digesting food (protein requiring the most energy compared to carbs and fats).

Other factors influence your metabolic rate as well (genetics, age, gender, medical conditions, etc.), but you have much more control over your TEA, NEAT, and TEF, so we're going to focus on those components. We'll dive deeper into them soon, but first: your total body mass is split into two categories: **fat** and **lean body mass (LBM)**. Fat is excess energy stored by your body. Lean body mass is everything in the body that is not fat—muscles, bones, organs, etc.

Your body is mostly made up of lean body mass, which is the main reason LBM has the bigger effect on your metabolic rate. And while there are some things you can control about your lean body mass, there are several you can't. Take your height, for example. Someone who is six feet tall, all else equal, will have much more lean body mass, and therefore a higher metabolic rate, than someone who is five feet tall. Their taller body just needs more energy to function. This applies whether they're at rest or moving. It takes more energy for larger bones, muscles, and organs to function. And it takes more energy to move a larger body vs. a smaller one. That means a taller person can eat more calories than a shorter person without gaining fat. Yes, it sucks for short people. Jordan is five feet four and complains about this daily.

Some people are also just genetically lucky in that their bodies are super efficient at burning calories and building muscle. The opposite is also true: some people have genetic factors that make their RMR slower, which makes it harder for them to build muscle.

Before you call it quits and think your body is working against you . . . stop. Just because you aren't among the "genetic elite" doesn't mean you can't lose weight, get stronger, build muscle, and be more defined. You can. You just have to put in a little bit of effort and stop having a weekly pity party because Sheryl at the office loses weight more easily than you. While there are some things that are a little bit outside of your control, the vast majority of the weight loss process is in your control (which is great news). There is a tremendous amount you can do to improve your body composition. And spoiler: none of it is tied to detox teas, fat-burning pills, or anything else someone may be trying to sell you.

What You Can Control about Your Metabolic Rate

The best thing you can do to improve your metabolism is to take the right actions. You can lift weights to build more muscle. You can exercise and move more frequently. You can improve your nutrition and eat more protein. It's easier said than done (and we'll continue to give you practical, easy-to-implement strategies), but these are three of the most important factors affecting your metabolism, and you have a tremendous amount of control over each of them. Let's discuss in more detail.

Build Muscle

The more you weigh (i.e., the more body mass you have), the greater your metabolic rate, which means you will burn more calories at rest. Now, you could increase your weight by gaining fat, but we're going to assume that's not your goal. Because increasing your body fat to increase your metabolic rate is like asking your boss to lower your salary so you can pay less in taxes—not the brightest idea. The more practical strategy is to focus on getting stronger and building more muscle. Not only will you feel and perform better, but muscle is more metabolically active than fat (which is a fancy way of saying muscle burns more calories than fat).

Having said all of that, there are two important points to consider. First and foremost, many women (and some men) don't like the idea of building muscle because they don't want to get "too big and bulky." Listen. Building muscle is hard. Very hard. And not lifting weights because you don't want to get too big and bulky is like never driving over the speed limit because you don't want to become a professional race-car driver. Believe us when we tell you that you aren't going to accidentally get too big and muscle-y. You will, however, get stronger and more defined. The "toned" look most people are looking for is only possible if you have enough muscle mass to begin with. Later on we'll give you a workout plan optimized to get you stronger and build muscle but, for now, suffice to say building muscle will both increase your metabolism and get you more defined.

Second, while increasing your muscle mass does increase your metabolism, most people massively overestimate how many extra calories their body is burning. Generally speaking, 1 pound of fat will burn 3 calories per day, whereas 1 pound of muscle burns about 6 calories per day. So, if you gain 10 pounds of muscle over the course of the next year (which would be amazing, by the way), your metabolic rate would increase by about 60 calories per day.

It might not seem like much, but Dr. Nadolsky points out that the greater benefit of building muscle is what you can do with that muscle. "Gaining muscle will increase your metabolic rate, but it's not much more than what fat would do per pound," he confirms. "The real key is that once you have that muscle, you're able to move more. You'll be faster. You'll be able to lift heavier weights. And this all leads to burning more calories throughout the day."

Dr. Nadolsky's point leads us to the next big factor in boosting your metabolic rate—movement.

Move More

This is where the **non-exercise activity thermogenesis (NEAT)** comes in. Remember, NEAT is the number of calories your body burns from any and all movement that isn't planned exercise (including things like fidgeting, foot tapping, raking leaves, washing the dishes, etc.). NEAT has a surprisingly significant effect on how many calories you burn every day and, depending on the individual, can range anywhere from 200 to 900 extra calories burned daily. Genetics do play a role in your NEAT, but it also varies based on how much you move. Odds are you knew "that kid" in school who was constantly fidgeting, running up and down the hallways, tapping his fingers on the desk, and behaving like a cracked-out fourteen-year-old. He had a high NEAT and was burning hundreds of extra calories a day simply because he was moving so much.

The cracked-out fourteen-year-old kid might have a genetically high NEAT. But regardless of your genetics you can deliberately increase your NEAT to get the same metabolic effect. For example, instead of taking the elevator, take the stairs. Instead of parking close to the grocery store, park in the farthest available spot. Instead of sitting down while you talk on the phone, go for a walk. It might not sound like much, but small changes like these done consistently make a huge difference, especially since for many of us, a normal workday is so sedentary. If you mostly sit at a desk all day, drive to and from work, and finish the day at home on the couch, your NEAT might be closer to 200 calories, which means it's your responsibility to take control and deliberately move more to increase it.

Myth: High-Intensity Cardio Is Best for Fat Loss

High-intensity cardio isn't bad. When used appropriately, there are many benefits, especially when it comes to athletic performance. The issue is, many coaches and fitness marketers say high-intensity cardio (e.g., sprints) is better for fat loss than low-intensity cardio (e.g., walking), and that isn't true.

The main reason people believe high-intensity cardio is best is due to something called excess post-exercise oxygen consumption (EPOC), which is a fancy way of saying your body will continue to burn extra calories from that workout for up to 48 hours after you've finished. Which is true. Your body will continue to burn extra calories for up to 48 hours after a bout of high-intensity cardio. But what these coaches and marketers won't tell you is that the number of extra calories you'll burn is painfully inconsequential, to the tune of about 40–80 extra calories burned . . . which means, congratulations, you burned off enough to eat nearly an entire small apple. Whoop-de-doo.

Again, there are many benefits of high-intensity cardio, and we aren't against it at all (especially for athletes). But when it comes to fat loss, we prefer emphasizing low-intensity cardio. Reasons being:

1. Low-intensity cardio is far less stressful on your joints/tendons/ligaments/etc., so if you have a lot of weight to lose, low-intensity cardio is much safer and less likely to cause an injury.

2. Since low-intensity cardio is less stressful on your body, you won't get nearly as hungry after doing it (whereas high-intensity cardio almost always leads to significantly more hunger).

3. This is often overlooked, but high-intensity cardio is more psychologically demanding and requires far more mental energy, willpower, and grit. This means you are much more likely to actually complete that two-mile low-intensity walk while listening to an audiobook than twenty high-intensity treadmill sprints (all the while hoping you don't misstep and get blasted off the treadmill in front of everyone at the gym).

If you enjoy high-intensity cardio, by all means, do it. Just remember you don't *need* to do high-intensity cardio, and it certainly isn't better than low-intensity cardio for fat loss.

Prioritize Protein

This is where the **thermic effect of food (TEF)** comes in. And by this point in the book you've already read so much about the importance of protein your eyes might bleed if we talk about it again. So we'll leave it at this: TEF is the energy required by your body to process a given food. Protein has the highest TEF compared to all other macronutrients, which means your body burns more calories processing protein than it does any other macro. In short, prioritizing protein in your diet gives your body a "metabolic advantage" so you can keep your metabolism as high as possible for as long as possible.

This is it. This is the not-so-sexy truth. People endlessly

look for tips, tricks, and strategies to increase their metabolism, but the reality lies in these three things: build muscle (lean body mass), move more (thermic effect of activity), and prioritize protein (thermic effect of food). Yes, other factors impact your metabolism as well (e.g., genetics). But you have control over the three most important factors that affect it, and if you take our advice, you will dramatically improve your metabolism and overall progress.

Exercise Several Times per Week

Most people think going crazy in the gym for an hour, trying to burn as many calories as possible during their 60-minute workout, is the best way to accelerate fat loss. The truth is: this planned exercise activity (TEA) makes up the smallest percentage of your total calorie burn (5 percent) compared to TEF (10 percent), NEAT (15 percent), and BMR (70 percent), which make up a combined 95 percent of your total calorie burn. With that in mind, exercise several times per week for the health and strength benefits, but don't rely on it as a primary way to increase your metabolism.

You Won't Damage Your Metabolism (and Here's Why)

Scroll through Instagram fitness accounts and it won't be long before you find a half-naked "influencer" warning you of the "dangers of metabolic damage." They'll tell you losing weight is bad because it permanently and irreversibly damages your metabolism. They'll say eating too few calories will put your body into "starvation mode," which is why you can't lose weight. And they'll cap the post off with a pitch to join their brand-new online coaching program that, of course, has only two spots left.

First and foremost, they have way more than two spots left. Second, the odds of you actually damaging your metabolism are so overwhelmingly minuscule it's laughable. We asked Dr. Nadolsky for his medical opinion on the matter, and he agrees. Yes, your metabolism can *slightly* slow down as you lose weight, but just because your metabolism slows down does *not* mean your metabolism is damaged. Not to mention, in order to permanently damage your metabolism, you would have to go to such outrageous extremes of near-starvation for such long periods of time that the vast majority of people (us included) would never get anywhere close.

If you're wondering why it's normal for your metabolism to slow down when you lose weight, remember when we spoke about body mass and how the bigger you are the more energy it takes to complete everyday activities? The same concept applies to both weight loss and weight gain. If you gain weight, for example (be it muscle or fat), your metabolism will increase in order to support that extra body mass. But we're assuming you don't want to gain body fat just so you can increase your metabolism; that would be stupid. Similarly, as you lose weight, your metabolism will decrease—not because it's "damaged" but because you have less total body mass and, consequently, require less energy to fuel your daily activities.

Remember, fitness marketers do everything in their power to confuse and scare you with the hope that you will feel so lost and out of control that you'll purchase one of their programs or products. Making you believe your metabolism is "damaged" is one of the many ways they'll do this. Don't fall for the hype. Don't let them get to you. Fat loss is simple (not easy). And as long as you stick to the principles we teach in this book, you will succeed.

"Starvation Mode" Is Not a Thing

We'll say it again: it is *normal* for your metabolism to slow down as you lose weight. And as we've mentioned on nearly every page since the first of this book, it's also normal for your weight loss to slow down and seemingly stall out because, as you know, you aren't going to lose weight every day or even every week. But when that inevitably happens, many people worry they've dieted to the point of "starvation mode." This is the asinine notion that if you don't eat enough calories, your body will somehow magically fight against you and hold on to more body fat. We understand why so many people fall for this myth (both of us did in the beginning of our fitness journeys), but it's not true. It does not exist. No one ever, in the history of ever, got fat from eating too little.

So what's going on? Why do people think they're in starvation mode when they swear up and down they're hardly eating anything and still aren't losing weight? The answer is because when they're on point with their diet, they're essentially starving themselves. They're barely eating more than carrot sticks and stalks of celery throughout the day. They don't allow themselves to indulge in any treats, nor do they let themselves go out with friends or colleagues after work. They're relentlessly strict with their nutrition (usually Monday to Thursday) in the hopes of losing as much weight as possible as quickly as possible.

When the weekend comes, however, they inevitably binge. They can't hold themselves back anymore, and since they starved themselves all week, they think they deserve time to indulge. The issue is, they eat way more than they think they do. And from Friday to Sunday, they easily inhale more than enough calories to offset the calorie deficit they created during the week. Bottom line, they're eating more than they think they are. And if they adopted a less restrictive, more sustainable approach that allowed them to enjoy their favorite foods in moderation throughout the week, they wouldn't feel the need to binge and overdo it every weekend.

This isn't the only time people think they're in starvation mode. Some people do this "binge-restrict" cycle on a daily basis (restrict all day, binge at night). And other people honestly think they're barely eating, but if they actually tracked their food intake (even for 3–5 days), they'd see their portions are significantly bigger than they thought and they're mindlessly snacking throughout the day without realizing it. So the next time Janice at the office tries convincing you that you aren't losing weight because you're in "starvation mode," kindly ask Janice how many people she knows who got fat from eating too little. Or how many prisoners of war got fat from eating too little. Or how many people who've suffered from anorexia got fat from eating too little.

Starvation mode is a myth. And it ends here.

Having said all of that, there *is* a process known as **metabolic adaptation** that's worth discussing.

First and foremost, metabolic adaptation is normal. It's not weird or unexpected or bad. It's a normal part of the process after losing a significant amount of weight. Now, without going into excruciating detail, metabolic adaptation refers to the reduction in your metabolic rate after losing a lot of weight.

For example, let's say we've got two men of the same height and who both weigh 185 pounds. Man 1 has weighed 185 pounds most of his adult life, whereas Man 2 previously weighed 285 pounds but lost 100 pounds over the past three years by following the exact principles laid out in this book. Please give Man 2 a round of applause to show him your support. You might assume that since both men are the same height and weight, they would have the same metabolic rate. This is where metabolic adaptation comes into play.

In reality, Man 2 would likely have a lower metabolic rate than Man 1 because as he lost 100 pounds his metabolic rate would experience a natural decline. Again, it's not bad or weird or unexpected. It's a normal part of losing a significant amount of weight. And as Dr. Nadolsky explains, "The problem is that people tend to get hyper-focused on this happening, when there's really a very small difference in your overall calorie burn. It can be anywhere from a 0 percent adaptation, up to a 10 percent to 20 percent adaptation." Even on the very high end, he points out, "it can mean the difference between having an extra snack throughout the day or not having one."

Dr. Nadolsky also clarifies that metabolic adaptation is more likely to occur with higher amounts of weight loss. Someone who loses 10–30 pounds (roughly speaking) is less likely to experience metabolic adaptation than someone who loses 100 pounds or more. So if Man 1's metabolic rate is 2,500 calories/day, Man 2's might be 2,200 calories/day. Which certainly isn't insignificant, but it's definitely not something to worry about like the half-naked Instagram influencer would have you believe.

6

Calorie Cycling for Fat Loss

By this point in the book, you know that in order to lose fat you need to be in a calorie deficit. And in Chapter 9 we're going to show you how to calculate how many calories you need to eat in order to be in a sustainable calorie deficit. Before we do, though, it's important to understand that there are many ways to structure your calorie intake throughout the week to make your regimen more enjoyable and easier to sustain over the long term. This is where calorie cycling comes into play.

At its core, calorie cycling is a fancy way of saying "On some days you eat more calories and on other days you eat fewer calories." We're going to explain the different ways you can use calorie cycling to your advantage, but don't overthink it—calorie cycling is simply a way of splitting your week into "high-" and "low-" calorie days.

How It Works

If you've ever worried about ruining all your progress because you accidentally went over your calories on any given day, pay attention because this section's for you. This is also why people do so well with calorie cycling. Because you don't need to eat the same amount of calories every day in order to lose fat. In our experience, we've found cycling between high- and low-calorie days will help you be more successful because it gives you an opportunity to be more flexible with your nutrition and enjoy your favorite foods while continuing to lose fat.

Here's how it works:

Let's say, for example, your daily calorie allotment is 1,800 calories. Most people think they've screwed up and ruined the day as soon as they hit 1,801 calories. This is also why calorie counting gets a bad reputation, because people think they need to be outrageously meticulous and precise in order to succeed.

You don't.

Rather than fixating on your daily calorie allotment, we want you to look at your *weekly* calorie allotment. So, using the above example, instead of 1,800 calories *per day*, you have an allotment of 12,600 calories *per week* (1,800 × 7 = 12,600). You can now distribute those calories however you want, as long as you've hit about 12,600 calories at the end of the week.

Again, you don't need to be perfect. It's not like eating 4 calories over your target would ruin your progress. Heck, you could eat 1,000 calories over your weekly target and still make progress. Anyone who says "Calorie counting doesn't work because you have to be meticulously precise" has no clue what they're talking about (and they are probably trying to sell you their revolutionary new "intuitive eating" hand-book).

Think of it like using the speedometer on your car. You don't need to know *exactly* how fast you're going down to the decimal point to see if you're under the speed limit. A quick glance at the speedometer will tell you if you're in the appropriate range. The same goes for calorie counting. You don't need to hit your exact calorie target in order to lose body fat. As long as you're in an appropriate range (which we'll explain in Chapter 9), you will consistently lose weight.

Calorie Cycling Strategies

Keep in mind that you don't *need* to calorie cycle. Many of our clients do well eating the same number of calories every day (we call this the "straight deficit"). They love the simplicity in this approach. People with predictable schedules often prefer the straight deficit since they can consistently plan when and what they eat.

But whatever your day looks like, sometimes you might want to mix things up. Or maybe you like the idea of having several days throughout the week when you can eat significantly more calories. That's why we love calorie cycling. Not because it's inherently "better" for fat loss, but because most people think they need to starve themselves in order to lose body fat. And, with calorie cycling, losing weight becomes significantly easier, more sustainable, and enjoyable knowing you can eat way more calories a few days every single week.

We've found two calorie cycling strategies that work especially well for us and our clients—the Alternate Deficit and the Weekend Warrior.

The Alternate Deficit

This is our personal favorite. You simply alternate between high-calorie and low-calorie days throughout the week. So let's say your daily calorie target is 1,800. Instead of doing a straight 1,800 every day, you could have four low days and three high days, spread throughout the week in any combination that works best for you. That could be four days of eating about 1,650 calories and three days of eating about 2,000 calories, in which you alternate these targets every other day.

To illustrate, using this example your week might look like this:

High Days (2,000 Calories): Tuesday, Thursday, Saturday
Low Days (1,650 Calories): Monday, Wednesday, Friday, Sunday

Many people ask if it matters how you schedule your "high" and "low" calorie days relative to your workouts. Should your workout days always be higher calorie and your rest days always be lower calorie? Or does it not make a difference? We'll talk more about your strength training and workouts in Chapter 10, but we will say that many of our clients do prefer higher calorie days on workout days because they've noticed that's when they tend to be most hungry. But if it works better for you to have lower calorie days on any of your training days, it's totally fine and won't ruin your progress (just make sure you hit your protein requirements, which we'll cover in Chapter 9).

The Weekend Warrior

This is a variation of the Alternate Deficit but done with the specific intent of making your weekends more enjoyable by stacking your three high-calorie days on Friday, Saturday, and Sunday. This way you can have more leeway on the weekends, dine out with friends and family, and enjoy eating more calories without worrying about ruining your progress. However, Monday to Thursday will then be relatively low-calorie days, so if you choose this approach, make sure that's realistic for you. Many people enjoy the Weekend Warrior because they tend to eat less during the week anyway and find the weekends to be where they struggle most with their nutrition. If this sounds like you, the Weekend Warrior might be worth giving a shot.

Looking again at our 1,800-calorie daily target (which adds up to 12,600 calories for the week), you might go Weekend Warrior and aim for roughly 1,500 daily calories Monday through Thursday, and then 2,200 daily calories on Friday, Saturday, and Sunday.

To illustrate, your week might look like this:

High Days (2,200 Calories): Friday, Saturday, Sunday
Low Days (1,500 Calories): Monday, Tuesday, Wednesday, Thursday

Keep in mind, if you use the Weekend Warrior approach, your weight *will* be heavier at the beginning of the week. It's not bad or weird or a sign that you're gaining fat. As we spoke about in Chapter 3, you're simply heavier because you ate more food over the weekend so, naturally, you'll weigh more. By Thursday and Friday you'll see your weight come back down, and week to week you'll notice a consistent downward trend.

Remember, even if your weekends allow for several hundred more calories per day, it doesn't take much to overdo it. The purpose of the higher calorie days isn't to justify untamed binge-eating. It's to give yourself the opportunity to enjoy some of your favorite foods in moderation while continuing to lose body fat. For that reason, we strongly recommend tracking your calories during the weekend as well. There is a common misconception that if you track your calories perfectly during the week, you can take the weekends off and still make consistent progress. Having cumulatively worked with thousands of clients, we can tell you that idea is patently false. People who were asked to estimate how many calories they ate over the course of the day underestimated by an astounding 50 percent. That means those who guessed they had consumed 1,500 calories had actually eaten 3,000.[*]

We're not saying you'll blow all your progress if you happen to miss a day of tracking. We *are* saying, however, that if you consistently track your calories during the weekdays

---

[*] S. W. Lichtman et al., "Discrepancy between Self-Reported and Actual Caloric Intake and Exercise in Obese Subjects," *New England Journal of Medicine*, U.S. National Library of Medicine, December 31, 1992, https://pubmed.ncbi .nlm.nih.gov/1454084/.

but never on the weekends, odds are you're going to radically underestimate how many calories you're eating. This is one of the main reasons so many people struggle to lose weight and can't figure out why. They swear up and down they're doing everything "right" during the week (which they are) and just "somewhat indulging" over the weekend. The problem is, since they weren't tracking their weekend, what they thought was "somewhat indulging" actually meant eating thousands of calories more than they realized.

Take, for example, a Friday night dinner at your favorite Mexican restaurant (which we love, by the way, and do several times each month). You grab a seat, munch on some warm tortilla chips and a bowl of freshly made guac, and order the frozen mango margarita. Because that's what you're supposed to do when you go to your favorite Mexican restaurant. But, before you know what happened, you've polished off two baskets of tortilla chips and enough guac to feed a family of four, and you're debating whether you want a second margarita. You've inhaled 1,400 calories, you're already full, and dinner hasn't even been served yet. You order the chicken fajitas, eat the entire plate (chicken, rice, sour cream, guac, beans, and all three tortillas) even though you weren't hungry for any of it, then nod your head when the waiter asks if you'd like to take a look at the dessert menu. You decide to get several desserts (churros, flan, and fried ice cream) and share with everyone at the table so you can all have a few bites of everything. Moderation. Once the meal is over you scan the table, trying to calculate how many calories you've eaten, thinking, *That couldn't have been more than 1,000 calories. . . . I'll log it as 1,200 just to be safe.* Meanwhile, your body is processing the 4,500 calories you just polished off (and that doesn't include however many calories you ate earlier that day).

This is why it's so important to track your calories, not just on the weekdays when you're doing things "perfectly," but also on the weekends. That way you can get an honest and objective idea of how consistent you're actually being with your nutrition.

Client Spotlight

Calorie Cycling on a Crazy Schedule

Kim's schedule is insane. She's a mom to three teens, volunteers heavily at her church, and is an online fitness coach with hundreds of clients around the world. No two days are ever the same. Sometimes her schedule revolves around driving kids to activities, doing laundry, and running church events. Other days she's on back-to-back calls with clients across four continents.

But, despite the chaos, she's figured out how to hit her calorie goals by calorie cycling around the ups and downs.

"I do three high-calorie days a week and four low-calorie days," she shared. "I never have a set schedule. So, on Sunday night, I look at my week ahead and pick my high days and my low days based on what I have going on. If I have a social engagement or I'm going out to dinner, I'll plan my high days around those events."

Kim also plans her food ahead of time—to a point.

"I'm not a huge meal prepper. I'm not going to spend three hours on Sunday cooking for the week and putting all my meals in nice, tidy Tupperware. That's not how my life works. But I do spend time once a week figuring out what food I need to get into my house, and what I need to keep out, so I can reach my goals."

Kim also pre-logs her meals into an app the night before so she doesn't have to think about it throughout the day. And she makes sure she actually likes the meals she plans to eat. Then, as the day goes on, she just adjusts her food log if she decides she wants something different. "Pre-logging meals takes less than five minutes once you get used to doing it—especially if you know you already have the foods you need at home."

7

Rapid Fat Loss 101

Losing weight, especially 50–100+ pounds, can feel like an impossible task. No matter how badly you want to lose it, it's easy to get overwhelmed thinking about how far you have to go and how difficult the journey is going to be. This is why an initial rapid fat loss protocol can be a more effective strategy than beginning with a moderate calorie deficit; because starting with a brief rapid fat loss phase, and losing weight very quickly from the beginning, proves you *can* do this and it *is* actually working. Getting to a point at which you're happy and excited about slow and steady progress is the ultimate goal because that is more sustainable in the long term. But if you don't believe in your ability to succeed from the very beginning, a brief rapid fat loss protocol can dramatically increase your self-efficacy and show you have the ability to succeed—and keep going.

Before we begin, it's important to clarify this chapter is *not* meant for people who want to lose 10–20 pounds of body fat for aesthetic purposes. If that's your goal, you are infinitely better off using a slower, more sustainable approach—Chapter 9 will have more specific instructions for that.

This chapter is for people who have at least 50–100+ pounds of body fat to lose, have struggled with their weight (physically, mentally, and emotionally) for many years, and are seriously concerned about the health risks of staying at their current body fat. The rapid fat loss protocols outlined in this chapter are in no way, shape, or form a long-term strategy. They are solely meant to be used for a brief period of time to help people with a very high body fat percentage improve their health as quickly as possible while simultaneously increasing their motivation and self-confidence. This way they can continue with a more sustainable approach once the rapid fat loss phase is over.

This is where self-efficacy comes in. Remember, self-efficacy is a person's belief in themselves to accomplish a given task. A lot of research has been done on how improving someone's self-efficacy can radically improve not only their ability to succeed in a given task but also their overall confidence and self-worth. The benefits of high self-efficacy are invaluable. With that said, let's get into the rapid fat loss protocol.

Six Steps to Structure Your Rapid Fat Loss Protocol

We've broken down the most important parts of a successful rapid fat loss protocol into six steps. Here's how it works:

Step 1: Set your time frame.

There's no need to do a rapid fat loss protocol for more than 30 days. And that's an absolute maximum. In our experience, somewhere between 7 and 21 days (1–3 weeks) is the optimal time frame for rapid fat loss. The more body fat you have to lose, the longer your rapid fat loss phase can be. Either way, **do not** make the mistake of thinking you're a special butterfly and can do it for longer than 30 days; 1–3 weeks is plenty.

Step 2: Set your calorie target.

Multiply your goal body weight by 8 to get your rapid fat loss calorie target. We'll discuss everything you need to know about your "goal weight" and how to set it appropriately in Chapter 9. But, for now, suffice to say your goal body weight is simply the weight at which you would no longer want to lose more fat. To illustrate, let's say your goal body weight is 150 pounds. $150 \times 8 = 1{,}200$ calories. That would be your calorie intake for the duration of your rapid fat loss phase. You can use a lower or higher multiplier of your choosing, but we don't recommend going lower than 6 times your goal weight. That is already *very* low, and anything less is likely to do more harm than good. Generally speaking, the more body fat you have, the lower you can set your rapid fat loss multiplier. So someone who is 300 pounds with 55 percent body fat could multiply their goal weight by 6, whereas someone who is 225 pounds with 40 percent body fat would likely do better multiplying their goal weight by 8 (assuming both have a similar goal weight).

Step 3: Set your protein target.

Your goal body weight is your daily protein target in grams. So, if your goal weight is 150 pounds, aim for 150 grams of protein per day. You can do more, but it will be difficult since your calorie target is already very low. Either way, make sure you're hitting your minimum protein target daily, especially during a rapid fat loss phase, because you want to do everything possible to maintain your muscle mass and stay as full as possible. You'll still work out a few days a week (see Chapters 10–13 for more on this), but it will be at a much lower intensity to compensate for the reduction in calories.

Step 4: Decide when to start.

The best time to start a rapid fat loss protocol is right at the beginning of your fat loss phase. Many people make the mistake of radically reducing calories when they notice their weight loss slow down after they've already been in a calorie deficit for a while. **Do not make this mistake.** It's normal for your weight loss to slow down as you continue to lose weight. And radically reducing calories at that point will increase the risk of losing muscle mass and decrease the sustainability of your weight loss. If you want to try a rapid fat loss protocol, do it right at the beginning of your fat loss phase when your motivation is at its peak. This way you'll lose a significant amount of body fat very quickly, and as your motivation begins to dwindle (which it *always* does), you can increase your calories to a more sustainable, enjoyable calorie deficit.

Step 5: Make a plan for what comes next.

It's not enough to understand that rapid fat loss is a short-term strategy. You also need a clear-cut plan for what you'll do once the rapid fat loss phase is over and a hard deadline for when you'll make the switch. One of the most common reasons people fail with rapid fat loss is because they don't have an exit plan. And even when they do have an exit plan, they often ignore it and try to extend the rapid fat loss phase longer than they should. This inevitably leads to a massive binge and regaining everything they worked so hard to lose. Before you begin your rapid fat loss phase, you *must* know the exact date on which you'll switch to a more sustainable calorie deficit, as well as exactly how many calories you'll be eating once rapid fat loss is over.

Step 6: Understand it's not supposed to be easy.

Fat loss isn't fun or easy even in a sustainable calorie deficit. It's never easy when you have to restrict or limit yourself from anything in life (especially when that means reducing your total calories). But, like most things in life, no one ever regrets pushing through something hard when they know the end result is worth the struggle. That being said, rapid fat loss is significantly harder than sustainable fat loss. Your calories are much lower and, as a result, you'll need to be way more restrictive with your nutrition. Your hunger will increase and your energy will likely be lower. This is why your rapid fat loss phase is designed to be brief and not a long-term solution. So, if you decide to give rapid fat loss a shot, know that it's going to be significantly harder than a more sustainable, flexible approach.

The Ascending Caloric Schema

No matter how you do it, rapid fat loss is always going to be difficult. A significant reduction in calories is never going to be fun or easy, and anyone who says otherwise is either lying, trying to sell you something, or a combination of the two. That said, there is one way to make rapid fat loss a bit easier: the Ascending Caloric Schema.

As we've discussed, motivation is at its peak right when you start your fat loss phase. You're excited thinking about how great it will be to *finally* lose that weight, and you're motivated to do whatever it takes to get there. Eventually, though, as time goes on and as progress inevitably slows down, motivation quickly dwindles, and excitement is nowhere to be found. It is at this moment when most people think they need to drop their calories even further in order to keep making progress. This, of course, becomes increasingly unsustainable and unenjoyable, and it's only a matter of time before they call it quits and regain everything they worked so hard to lose.

The Ascending Caloric Schema reverses your natural instinct to decrease calories and, instead, has you increasing calories week over week. Instead of starting with higher calories and progressively lowering them over time, the Ascending Caloric Schema begins with your calories at their lowest (when your motivation is highest) and gradually increases your calories as your motivation and excitement naturally decline.

Remember, you'll still be in a calorie deficit even as you're increasing calories. Four weeks of rapid fat loss would look something like this:

Week 1: 8 × goal weight
Week 2: 9 × goal weight
Week 3: 10 × goal weight
Week 4: 11 × goal weight

Assuming you're consistent with these calories, you will see the most rapid weight loss in the first week. It will get progressively slower from there, but you will still make progress (and fast progress, at that). The great part about the Ascending Caloric Schema is that it's a built-in strategy moving you toward a more sustainable approach throughout the entire rapid fat loss phase. So, rather than suffering through outrageously low calories for an entire month, you progressively increase your calories (while staying in a calorie deficit), which allows you to quickly lose body fat and seamlessly transition into your sustainable calorie deficit immediately after.

Not to mention, if you do a traditional rapid fat loss protocol (not the Ascending Caloric Schema), your weight *will* temporarily spike up as you transition from very low calories to a more sustainable calorie deficit. With the Ascending Caloric Schema, however, you won't have such drastic changes in scale weight because you're progressively increasing calories week over week, which can help if you find yourself very emotionally affected by fluctuations in scale weight.

When you think about it, the Ascending Caloric Schema is another form of calorie cycling. While the methods of calorie cycling explained in the previous chapter work on day-to-day fluctuations in calories, the same principles apply to the Ascending Caloric Schema on a week-to-week basis.

Regardless of whether or not you decide to use this rapid fat loss protocol, there are many lessons to be gleaned from this chapter. Notably, your motivation will always be highest at the beginning of a fat loss phase and will inevitably decline the longer you're in a calorie deficit. This is why it's critical to structure your diet in a way that allows you to sustain it long term, so you aren't relying on sheer willpower to force your way through each and every day. This is why, using the Ascending Caloric Schema, we progressively increase your calories over time. It's also the reason we recommend a rapid fat loss phase should never last more than 30 days. By carefully following these guidelines, you will be able to lose fat and keep it off for the rest of your life without feeling like you're suffering through every waking moment.

8

Your Nutrition Toolbox

There are two main reasons people struggle to lose weight and keep it off forever. The first reason is they don't know what to do. They aren't sure which foods they should (or shouldn't) eat. They don't know which exercise is "best." They don't know what plan they should follow. That's the main reason we wrote this book: to eliminate any and all confusion and give you the knowledge and tools to help you succeed.

The second reason people struggle to lose weight has nothing to do with knowledge. They know what to do. They know how many calories to eat (as we outline in Chapter 9). They know how to emphasize protein in their diet (as we discussed in Chapter 4). They have an incredible workout program to follow (as we give you in Chapters 12 and 13). And they know, if they put in the time and effort, it can be done. But they find it difficult to take all of this knowledge and put it into practice. Maybe it's because they find themselves getting hungry all the time. Maybe they're discouraged by their lack of weight loss. Maybe it's because they struggle with sugar cravings. Maybe it's because they don't know how to handle dining out at social events. It could be any number of these or other possibilities.

In this chapter we're going to discuss some of the most common struggles people have with their nutrition and how to overcome them. By the end of this chapter, you won't just know *what* to do to achieve your goals, you'll also have strategies to help you take action even when (and especially if) you might not want to.

Why Am I Not Losing Weight?

If you've tried counting calories and still haven't been able to lose weight (no matter how few calories you ate), we're going to explain why and how to fix that going forward.

We'll start by reminding you: if you aren't losing weight, it's *not* because you're eating "too little." We spoke about the myth of "starvation mode" ad nauseum in Chapter 5, so if you need a refresher on why no one ever got fat from eating too little, flip back a few chapters and reread that section.

With that out of the way, the main reason people struggle to lose weight (even when they swear up and down they're in a calorie deficit) is because . . . wait for it . . . they aren't actually in a calorie deficit. Before you throw this book across the room and impulse buy fat-burning pills on Amazon, we aren't saying you're lying. And we're not saying you aren't working incredibly hard. What we are saying—and what decades of the best scientific research has consistently shown[*]—is people who struggle to lose weight dramatically underestimate how many calories they're eating, even when they think they're tracking calories accurately.

Sometimes this comes from underestimating portion sizes. Other times it's from tracking calories during the week but not the weekends. Other times it's from tracking

---

[*] S. W. Lichtman et al., "Discrepancy between Self-Reported and Actual Caloric Intake and Exercise in Obese Subjects," *New England Journal of Medicine*, U.S. National Library of Medicine, December 31, 1992, https://pubmed.ncbi.nlm.nih.gov/1454084/.

calories during your meals but forgetting to track the small snacks (licks, bites, and tastes) you eat throughout the day. And other times it's from tracking meticulously for 1–2 weeks followed by several weeks of hardly tracking at all. In each of these examples, it's not a lack of effort causing you to stall in weight loss; it's a lack of awareness. We know you're working hard, and our job is to now help you become more aware of how many calories you're actually eating so you can start making the progress you deserve.

For example, here is a quick list of some of the most commonly missed/untracked calories:

- **Make sure you track** the cream you poured in your coffee (150 cals)
- **Make sure you track** the orange juice you drank on the way to work (200 cals)
- **Make sure you track** the hefty pour of Italian dressing you use to top your salad (300 cals)
- **Make sure you track** the random handful(s) of mixed nuts you had throughout the day (250 cals)
- **Make sure you track** the oil you used on the pan to stir-fry chicken and veggies (240 cals)
- **Make sure you track** the chicken nuggets you ate off your child's dinner plate (175 cals)
- **Make sure you track** the glass of wine you had with dinner (150 cals)
- **Make sure you track** the two spoonfuls of cookie dough you ate while you were baking (300 cals)

In isolation, any one of these instances might not seem like much. But even just a few of them left untracked on a consistent basis can easily add up to well over 1,000 uncounted calories.

Now, here is a quick list of calories people may not be tracking accurately:

- **Make sure you weigh** your peanut butter. The peanut butter you eyeballed as 1.5 tablespoons is, unfortunately, closer to 4 tablespoons and more than double your projected calories.
- **Make sure you weigh** your avocado. While it's a great source of high-quality fat, it is *very* calorie dense and easy to underestimate and overeat.
- **Make sure you weigh** your meat and fish *before* you cook it. Without going into excruciating detail, you won't get an accurate measurement if you weigh your meat/fish after it's cooked because of the water lost through cooking. None of the calories are lost, but the weight changes due to the water loss. Weighing before cooking eliminates this variable and keeps your calories in check.

If you're struggling to lose weight and swear you're in a calorie deficit, but you haven't accurately weighed your food and tracked your calories for at least 30 days, odds are you aren't in a calorie deficit. Again, this isn't a lack of effort on your part, simply a lack of awareness. In the same way you'd seriously track your income and expenses if you wanted to get your finances in order, take 30 days to seriously track your calorie intake. We don't take it lightly when we say it could change your life forever and make losing weight and keeping it off both sustainable and enjoyable.

The other common reason people struggle to lose weight is because even when they're making incredible progress, they *think* it's not working. They think it should be happening faster. They think they aren't losing enough weight quickly enough and, as a result, they call it quits before they've even given themselves a chance to make extraordinary progress.

Remember, as we spoke about in Chapter 3, an average weight loss of 0.5–2 pounds per week is phenomenal. This doesn't mean you'll lose up to 2 pounds every single week for months on end. You probably won't. This means that when you look at your *average weight loss over time*, you'll see it falls somewhere between 0.5 and 2 pounds per week.

Some people might lose weight more quickly than you. Becky from accounting might lose 20 pounds in 4 weeks by following keto and completely eliminating carbs from her diet. *Stop comparing yourself to Becky.* Her progress is irrelevant to your progress. And who cares how much weight someone can lose in 4 weeks if they end up regaining it all (and more) soon after? Sustainable results come only with a sustainable mindset. And if the methods you're using to lose weight aren't sustainable, the results won't be sustainable.

Stop comparing yourself to other people and stop expecting rapid results.

Start being patient and start giving yourself the opportunity to succeed by not quitting at the first sign of difficulty.

Seven Ways to Stay Full in a Calorie Deficit

Hunger is, unfortunately, a normal part of being in a calorie deficit. You shouldn't be starving, nor should you constantly be thinking about food or when your next meal is going to be. But a little bit of hunger is normal and expected when you're trying to lose weight. The same works in reverse, by the way: when people try to gain weight and eat in a caloric surplus, they often have difficulty eating enough because their body downregulates or reduces hunger. Your body wants to stay exactly as it is (a process known as homeostasis). So, whether you deliberately increase or decrease calories, your body will respond by decreasing or increasing hunger respectively.

Having said that, we have a handful of easy-to-implement strategies you can use to keep hunger to a minimum. Some of them are based on the types of food you're eating. Others are based on when and how often you eat. And others are based on lifestyle habits that can dramatically improve your results. Keep in mind, none of these strategies in isolation will cause you to lose fat if you aren't in a calorie deficit. But once you are in a calorie deficit, these strategies will make fat loss significantly easier and more enjoyable.

1. Don't put yourself in an extreme calorie deficit.

You'll find your precise calorie guidelines in Chapter 9, and you'll notice they are not extremely low by any stretch of the imagination. In fact, many readers will think we've made a mistake because your calories are "too high." This is *not* a mistake, and your calories are *not* too high (so don't lower them before you've even given them a shot).

We deliberately keep your calories as high as possible because it is essential for sustainable fat loss. If you radically reduce your calories and put yourself in an extreme deficit for too long, the odds of you rebounding and gaining all the weight back (and more) radically increase. Use the calorie guidelines we provide you in Chapter 9, keep a low-to-moderate calorie deficit, and you'll find fat loss is significantly easier and more enjoyable than fitness marketers would have you believe.

Important note: If you qualify to use a rapid fat loss protocol as we outlined in Chapter 7, this is why we clearly say it should be a *maximum* of 30 days. And that is an absolute maximum.

2. Eat more fruits and vegetables.

Shocking, we know. You didn't buy this book to read another pair of fitness professionals telling you how important it is to eat fruits and veggies on a regular basis, so we aren't going to waste your time explaining why they're important. With that said, in recent years a few charlatans have told people to avoid eating them because the sugar is going to make you fat. That is false—and, frankly, one of the dumbest things we've ever heard. No one ever got fat from eating fruits or vegetables. If you're struggling with hunger, eat more fruits and veggies. We can't believe we live in a world in which this is a controversial thing to say.

For whatever it's worth, an entire pound of watermelon is only 140 calories. We'll say that again. An *entire pound* of watermelon is only 140 calories. So, if you find yourself getting hungry, you can fill up on a bowl of delicious watermelon without blowing past your calories. (And before you say, *"What about the sugar!?"* how many people do you know who got fat from eating watermelon?) Strawberries are only 150 calories for an entire pound. Mix a fistful of those into a bowl of Greek yogurt with some cinnamon on top and you've got yourself a delicious low-calorie and high-protein dessert. The list goes on and on.

However, it's worth taking a moment to examine fresh fruit vs. dried fruit. There's nothing inherently wrong with dried fruit if you want to eat it in moderation. But if your goal is to keep hunger to a minimum, dried fruit should not make up a significant portion of your diet because removing the water and some fiber from the fruit makes it substantially less filling for the same number of calories.

To illustrate why:

An entire pound of fresh mango is only 295 calories, whereas 1 pound of dried mango is 1,650 calories.
An entire pound of fresh pineapple is only 227 calories, whereas 1 pound of dried pineapple is 1,312 calories.
An entire pound of fresh apple is only 237 calories, whereas 1 pound of dried apple is 1,130 calories.

This is why fresh fruit is superior to dried fruit, especially when the goal is to reduce hunger. You can eat significantly more fresh fruit for, literally, a fraction of the calories of dried fruit.

3. Eat more protein.

We've said this before and we'll say it again: protein is critically important when you're trying to lose weight (and keep it off forever). It is far and away the most filling macronutrient, so eating at least 20–25 grams of protein per meal will not only help your muscles get stronger and more defined but also keep you fuller for longer.

4. Stay hydrated.

Drink. Drink water. Drink water consistently throughout the day. There's no need to overcomplicate this. Thirsty? Drink water. Hungry? Drink water. Your pee is starting to get dark? Drink water. No need to go overboard with it, but make sure you're staying hydrated because—aside from the obvious health and performance benefits—it's one of the easiest ways to mitigate hunger. Jordan prefers sparkling and Mike prefers still. Don't overcomplicate it. Just drink water.

5. Eat more fiber.

Lyle McDonald, the "godfather" of evidence-based nutrition, has called fiber "nature's broomstick." If you aren't sure what that means, we'll just say it's great for digestion and helping things move along as "effortlessly" as possible. It also helps lower cholesterol, control blood sugar, and, most relevant to this section, it helps you stay full on fewer calories.

This doesn't mean you should start wolfing down fiber-infused faux health bars (which are really just glorified candy) and expect to be full for hours on end. You'd quickly realize that simply infusing a bar with fiber isn't going to mitigate hunger. When we encourage you to eat more fiber, we want you to focus on whole, minimally processed sources, such as:

- Beans/lentils/chickpeas
- Oatmeal
- Berries
- Apples
- Avocado
- Almonds
- Potatoes
- Brown rice
- Green beans
- Eggplant
- And many more . . .

6. Strategize your meals.

If you really want to reduce your hunger, paying attention to the order in which you eat certain food groups within a single meal can be very helpful for filling up without overloading on calories. For example, if you begin your meal with vegetables (be it a salad, stir-fry, etc.), you'll quickly fill up on the lower-calorie, nutrient-dense options. From there, focusing on your proteins (chicken, salmon, etc.) is going to be your best bet because once you've finished your vegetables and protein, you're going to be significantly more full and satisfied than if you began with the carbs and fats (mac and cheese, bread and butter, etc.). From here, choose whichever foods you prefer. This way you can enjoy your favorite foods without going overboard.

Another strategy you can use pertains to the frequency and timing of your meals, which we'll discuss later in this chapter.

7. Sleep more.

If you're a parent of young children, you might have to let this one slide for a few more years. That doesn't mean you won't be able to lose fat (you will as long as you're in a calorie deficit). But there is no question that a lack of sleep makes many things in life considerably more difficult, and that includes fat loss. Generally speaking, at least 7–8 hours of sleep every night is going to help regulate your mood, energy, hunger, and performance. Recent research has also shown that a lack of sleep can make it significantly harder to build muscle. So, if your goal is not only to lose fat but also to get stronger and more defined, prioritizing sleep is essential.

Implementing these seven strategies will make losing weight significantly easier, more enjoyable, and sustainable in the long term. That said, remember, hunger is a normal part of the process. You shouldn't be starving or ravenous, but a little hunger is actually a good sign because it means you're in a calorie deficit and losing body fat. Use these strategies (and develop your own along the way) to mitigate hunger as much as possible. But remember, a bit of hunger isn't an emergency; it's just part of the process.

Intermittent Fasting

In recent years, intermittent fasting (IF) has joined the ranks of the most popular mainstream diet fads. Self-proclaimed gurus and experts love making unsubstantiated claims that intermittent fasting is the key to fixing your broken metabolism, balancing your hormones, and eliminating stubborn belly fat. Of course, these claims are always followed by an elaborate sales pitch leading you toward their brand-new, never-before-seen intermittent fasting course. Don't fall for the hype.

Intermittent fasting isn't bad or dangerous. In fact, it can be an effective tool to help you lose fat and keep you full while dieting. But it's important to understand that intermittent fasting is not inherently better than other meal timing strategies. For some people, intermittent fasting works very well, depending on your day-to-day schedule as well as your individual preferences. For others, however, it's not a good fit and can sometimes do more harm than good. The only way to know whether intermittent fasting is right for you is through trial and error to see how you respond. In the remainder of this section, we'll outline the essentials of intermittent fasting so you can decide if it's worth it for you to try.

What is intermittent fasting? The idea is simple: You break your day into two phases—your eating phase and your fasting phase. That's it. You're just setting predetermined times during which you're eating or not eating. The fasting phase usually begins once you've finished eating at the end of the day, and the eating phase begins when you break your fast the following day.

Based on the definition we just gave you, it's worth noting everyone does a form of intermittent fasting every day. Assuming you aren't waking up every hour to knock back a few chocolate chip cookies and Rice Krispies Treats, you're likely fasting at least 7–9 hours every night while you sleep. That's why it's called breakfast (*break* + *fast*), because you're *breaking* the night's *fast*. Feel free to use this fun fact to impress your friends and family.

There are many different forms of intermittent fasting, and we'll name a few of them. Just remember, regardless of the method, there is nothing uniquely better or superior about intermittent fasting. It's really just a fancy way of saying you skip breakfast (and maybe lunch). That's it.

The main benefits of intermittent fasting, specifically in regard to weight loss, are threefold:

- **Hunger Management:** You already know hunger is a normal part of being in a calorie deficit, but intermittent fasting may help you stay fuller by allowing you to eat larger meals. Rather than eating smaller meals spaced evenly throughout the day, intermittent fasting allows you to eat a couple of significantly bigger meals (albeit in a briefer time frame). If you enjoy eating bigger meals less frequently throughout the day, intermittent fasting might be great for you.
- **Good for Crazy Schedules:** This isn't relevant if you work a standard 9-to-5 desk job, but if you're constantly on

the go with very little time to sit down for regular meals, intermittent fasting can be an effective tool to help you stay organized with your meals and allow you to enjoy larger portions of food when you finally have time to sit down and eat. This tends to work incredibly well for late-night shift workers, regular travelers, and transportation workers.

- **Less Opportunity to Overeat:** Most people eat anytime they want, day or night. With intermittent fasting, however, you have predetermined times in which you're either eating or fasting. And since your eating window tends to be relatively brief (usually between 8 and 10 hours), you give yourself fewer opportunities to overeat simply by reducing the amount of time you're "allowed" to eat.

If you want to try intermittent fasting, you're more than welcome to set your own eating/fasting windows. If you would like more guidance and structure, however, we've outlined our personal favorite approach below.

16/8: The Leangains Method

This approach was popularized by nutritional consultant and personal trainer Martin Berkhan. Known in the fitness world as "the godfather of intermittent fasting," Martin brought intermittent fasting into mainstream conversations around fat loss and fitness in the early 2000s. His website, Leangains.com, and his book, *The Leangains*

Method, outline his comprehensive protocol for intermittent fasting.

The basic premise of the Leangains Method is to fast for 16 hours of the day (this includes sleep time) and eat during an 8-hour window. During your fasting window you'd only consume zero-calorie drinks like water, tea, or black coffee.

You can set your eating window to whatever times you want based on what works for you. Many of our clients choose to fast in the morning (i.e., skip breakfast), often because they aren't hungry for breakfast anyway, and they would prefer to eat bigger meals later in the day.

To illustrate, a sample day might look like this:

Wake Up: 7:00 a.m.
Fast: 7:00 a.m.–12:00 p.m.
First Meal: 12:00 p.m.
Second Meal: 4:00 p.m.
Last Meal: 7:00 p.m.
Fast Begins: 8:00 p.m.

If you find that 16 hours is too long to go without food, you can modify your fasting/eating windows to 14 hours fasting/10 hours eating or even 12 hours fasting/12 hours eating. This is not about enduring the longest possible fasting window. It's about finding a method that works best for you so you can introduce more structure to your calorie intake.

Berkhan was one of the first people to debunk the myth that eating six small meals a day would stoke your metabolic fire to help you lose fat. If it weren't for him, intermittent fasting would not be as popular as it is today.

Other Forms of Intermittent Fasting

There are many methods of intermittent fasting, but each one seems to become more extreme than the last.

- The Warrior Diet advocates a 20-hour daily fast followed by a 4-hour eating window.
- Eat Stop Eat recommends fasting for a full 24 hours a couple of times each week.
- Other "experts" promote severely long-term fasts ranging from 72 hours all the way up to a full week (or even longer).

You're more than welcome to look into each of these methods on your own. Just remember, a longer fasting window does not equate to better fat loss (especially if it causes you to binge-eat after every fast). As we've said, the 16/8 Leangains Method is our personal favorite and has consistently proven to be the most enjoyable and sustainable way to incorporate intermittent fasting into your life.

Everything we've said boils down to the fact that eating in a calorie deficit is the most important factor in losing fat. It doesn't matter if you do intermittent fasting or not. You have to be in a calorie deficit in order to lose fat. Period.

Client Spotlight

Intermittent Fasting—Love It, Hate It, Whatever

"I did not do well with intermittent fasting. I'd rather eat throughout the day, so I try to eat pretty frequently, and I like to eat first thing in the morning. When I tried intermittent fasting, I spent the whole morning thinking about food. And it felt like one more rule I had to follow."

—Jenny

"Intermittent fasting works really well to help me stay in a calorie deficit. I have a coffee around 8:00 or 9:00 a.m. to help curb my hunger, and then I eat my first meal of the day at around noon. At night I just stop eating whenever I want. I don't have this fear that the devil is going to come after me if I eat after my 8-hour window."

—Danny

"I tried intermittent fasting, but it just caused me to binge at night. I would skip breakfast, start eating later in the day, and I would just not stop eating. It didn't work for me."

—Lisa

"Intermittent fasting didn't work for me until I figured out the right timing. When I first tried it, I'd go to the gym in the morning and have my first meal at lunchtime. But I'd be physically crashing by then. I couldn't do anything until lunch. Then I tried to eat something small before working out, and it fixed the problem. It didn't take much food at all. Just eating a small cup of oatmeal before going to the gym stopped me from crashing later in the day."

—*Chris*

Myths and FAQs about Intermittent Fasting

There is a great deal of misinformation and confusion around the subject of intermittent fasting. In this section we're going to cover and dispel IF's most common myths so you understand how to use it and whether it's a good option for you.

Myth: Putting a splash of milk in your coffee ruins the fast.

Fact: Unfollow anybody who says you can't put milk in your coffee. No one ever got fat from putting some milk in their morning coffee. People do get fat, however, from knocking back several Mocha Frappuccinos a day, especially when they're filled with chocolate syrup, whipped cream, caramel drizzle, Oreos, and/or a couple of s'mores for good measure. As long as you're drinking actual coffee with just a splash of milk and not a trash can–sized tub of liquid dessert every day, you're good.

Question: Can I intermittent fast if I work out early in the morning?

Answer: If you want to, yes, you can. It won't ruin your progress if you don't eat immediately before/after training. But, candidly, we don't recommend it. Just because it won't "ruin" your progress doesn't mean it won't impact your progress. And there's no question that eating before and after training will improve your workout performance and recovery. With that said, if you work out early in the morning and aren't hungry enough to eat beforehand, that's not a problem. Just make sure you eat some protein and carbohydrates within 30–60 minutes after your workout is finished.

Myth: Intermittent fasting is dangerous for women.

Fact: If intermittent fasting were dangerous for women (or any human for that matter), we wouldn't have survived as a species. It's only in very recent years that we've been fortunate enough to have large quantities of food available to us whenever we want simply by opening up the pantry door. For the vast majority of our existence, humans would go long periods of time without eating between meals. So, no, intermittent fasting is not dangerous for women simply because they are women.

However, as we mentioned above, intermittent fasting is not for everyone. Longer fasting windows can lead to and perpetuate binge-eating for both men and women. So, if you find yourself struggling to control your food intake while intermittent fasting, stop immediately and go back to a more "traditional" eating pattern.

Question: Can you build muscle while intermittent fasting?

Answer: Yes, absolutely. Some people struggle to eat enough calories while intermittent fasting because they need to eat more in a brief period of time. But as long as your calorie and protein intakes are in check, and you're following a well-designed training program (like the ones we'll provide in Chapters 12 and 13), you will build muscle regardless of whether or not you intermittent fast.

The Jab Deficit

Many people struggle with being consistent in a calorie deficit because they don't see an end in sight. There's no "light at the end of the tunnel." They're working as hard as they possibly can to keep their calories in check, hit their workouts, prioritize sleep, etc., but they have no idea how long it's going to take to achieve their goals, which can be discouraging, to say the least. So, rather than plodding along, they give up and throw in the towel because the idea of staying in a calorie deficit for lord-knows-how-long is unbearable.

This is where the Jab Deficit comes into play. Rather than diving headfirst into a calorie deficit for "as long as it takes," you set a brief, predetermined period of time (2–4 weeks) to be 100 percent consistent in a calorie deficit. Once that time frame is up, you slightly increase calories to maintenance (the number of calories required to maintain your current bodyweight) for about 1–4 weeks to take a mini diet break and give yourself time to relax and gear up for another "jab" in a calorie deficit for 2–4 weeks. You can repeat this cycle as many times as you want until you achieve your goal.

The Jab Deficit doesn't work as quickly as continuing to be in a straight calorie deficit for a longer period of time. But just because it's not as fast doesn't mean it isn't as effective. If you know you're the person who won't be consistent in a long-term calorie deficit, using the Jab approach will likely get you better results than you've ever had before because, for the first time, you'll actually be 100 percent consistent for the brief periods you're in a calorie deficit. With that consistency you'll see real, visible progress. And, as a result, you'll get more motivated to stay consistent with each consecutive "jab."

The best part is that you don't need to consistently be in a calorie deficit for months on end. You can have brief periods of time (2–4 weeks) in which you choose to be 100 percent consistent in a deficit, followed by brief periods of time (1–4 weeks) in which you can deliberately bring yourself out of a calorie deficit and enjoy a few more calories so you aren't feeling overwhelmed or deprived.

Keep in mind, with the Jab approach your weight/measurements will go down during each jab but will stay the same or even slightly increase during each diet break. This is normal. It's not bad or unexpected or even necessarily fat gain. When you increase the amount of food you eat, of course you will weigh a bit more (as we discussed in Chapter 3). Not to worry. Keep following the formula and, resembling a downward staircase graph, you will continue to lose body fat slowly and surely without being overly restrictive.

Some people might think this approach is like taking two steps forward and one step back. Not a terrible analogy, but it isn't correct, so let's adapt it. The Jab Deficit is more like taking two steps forward, then pausing and standing right where you are to enjoy the view (and the extra calories that come with it). When you repeat this cycle several times over (two steps forward, pause, two steps forward, pause), you'll end up making great progress.

With the Jab Deficit, you'll quickly realize that being in a calorie deficit doesn't have to suck and this isn't a zero-sum game. You can do it slowly and steadily while enjoying your favorite foods in moderation.

What to Do If You're Hungry at the End of the Day

The day is almost over, you've already finished dinner, you've eaten your allotted calories for the day, and you're still hungry. What are you supposed to do? Is it okay to go over your daily calories so you don't go to bed hungry? Should you suck it up and deal with it? What should you do if this happens on a regular basis? That's what we're going to cover in this section.

First and foremost, and as we've mentioned, a little hunger is normal. It's not an emergency and, when your goal is fat loss, it's actually a good sign that you're in a calorie deficit and making progress.

Second, nothing is wrong with going over your calories every now and then. Just as no one ever made incredible progress by being in a calorie deficit for one day, no one ever lost all their progress by being in a calorie surplus for one day. So, if you happen to go over your calories because you were hungrier than usual, no big deal. Granted, if this is happening on a regular basis and preventing you from being in a calorie deficit week over week, you need to make a change, because you shouldn't be unbearably hungry. And if you consistently go over your allotted calories, you're not going to make the progress you want.

With that said, if you find yourself feeling hungry on a random night, here are some strategies to keep yourself full without blowing past your calories.

1. **Drink a zero-calorie beverage.** Water, seltzer, decaf tea or coffee, diet juice or soda . . . the options are limitless. Just pick one of your favorite zero-calorie drinks and enjoy. And if someone tells you "Diet soda makes you fat because it tricks your body into thinking it's real soda," never take nutrition advice from that person ever again because they have no idea what they're talking about.

2. **Eat fruit.** *gasp* Yes, this again. As crazy as it might sound, you could eat some fresh fruit to fill you up and satisfy your sweet tooth. Obviously chocolate tastes better, but if you're trying to hit your calories and want to fill up on something low-calorie, try snacking on some watermelon, strawberries, an orange, an apple, or any fruit you want.

3. **Add protein.** If you want something even more filling, include a low-calorie protein option. One of our favorite combos is strawberries with a bowl of Greek yogurt. It's sweet and filling, and the yogurt is high in protein. Beef jerky, cottage cheese, or a protein shake are also great options. Jump to the Appendix of this book for more high-protein, low-calorie food options.

4. **Brush your teeth.** This is going to sound weird, but it works. If you're getting hungry but don't want to eat more calories, brushing your teeth and getting that "minty fresh" feeling in your mouth can help quickly reduce hunger. We're not sure if it's physiological, psychological, or a combination of the two, but there's something about brushing your teeth that quickly diminishes the desire to eat more before you go to bed.

5. **Prioritize nutrient-dense foods during the day.** If you're consistently hungry at the end of the day, odds are you're eating too few calories and/or not prioritizing nutrient-dense foods during the day. Feel free to enjoy your favorite treats in moderation, but the vast majority of your diet should consist of whole, minimally processed, fresh foods. Not just because of the health benefits, but also because they keep you full for significantly fewer calories.

Whether you follow these strategies or not, it's important to remember no one ever got fat from going over their calories for a day, a week, or even a month. Progress (both forward and backward) takes an incredible amount of time and consistency. So, if you happen to go over your calories for one day, relax. It's not a big deal. Just get back on track the following day, prioritize nutrient-dense foods, and be as consistent as you possibly can.

How to Be Strategic with Food at Social Events

First and foremost, social events shouldn't be a burden on your nutrition goals. This book isn't about fitting life into your nutrition; it's about learning how to fit nutrition into your life. We want you to enjoy yourself when you go out with friends and family. We want you to be able to focus on the people in front of you rather than obsessing over what and how much you're going to eat. With that in mind, we understand going out to eat (especially if you do it on a regular basis) can make achieving your fitness goals more difficult. So, in this section, we're going to take the stress out of social events by giving you several strategies to help you stay on track while enjoying yourself.

1. **Save calories for later in the day.** If you know you have a dinner planned ahead of time, the easiest way to set yourself up for success is to reduce your calories earlier on so you have more wiggle room at the social event. Keep in mind, we're not suggesting you starve yourself all day leading up to dinner. That's stupid. But by eating fewer calories earlier in the day, you'll be able to eat more food at dinner. The key is to save as many calories as possible *without* starving yourself.

2. **Fill up on lean protein, fruits, and vegetables earlier in the day.** Expanding on point #1, if you're going to try to eat fewer calories during the day leading up to the social event, it makes sense to allocate the majority of your cal-

ories to lean protein and filling, high-fiber fruits and vegetables. Not only will this keep you full for fewer calories but it also helps you hit your protein intake earlier in the day so you can have more "fun foods" at dinner.

3. **Don't go in blind.** If you're going to a restaurant, spend a few minutes checking the menu online beforehand to get a sense of what you'd like to order. There's no reason to go in blind. If you know you'll have, say, 1,200 calories left for dinner, you can decide what you'll eat ahead of time so you don't wing it when you get there. If you do this early enough in the day, you can even plan your earlier meals accordingly. So, if you're dying for a sushi entrée that is about 1,000 calories and your daily target is 1,900, you can aim to cap your prior meals at 900 calories.

4. **Stick to the one-plate rule.** If you don't want to do any of the above, you can simply moderate your portion size by making sure everything you eat at dinner fits on one plate. This allows you to have fun and enjoy your favorite foods without going overboard and inhaling as much food as you possibly can. Obviously, tracking your calories as we outlined in points 1–3 will be more accurate. But if you prefer not to track calories so meticulously, this is a great option to keep your portions under control.

5. **Don't forget the alcohol.** Many people think alcohol must be off-limits if you're trying to lose weight. They're wrong. You can absolutely incorporate alcohol into your diet while losing weight, as long as you're in a calorie deficit. Just remember to include the calories you'll be consuming from alcohol into your total daily intake because,

whether *you* count them or not, calories always count. If you aren't sure how many calories are in a certain drink, use the Google machine.

This is by no means an exhaustive list of strategies. The more you practice, the better you'll get at finding what works best for you and coming up with your own strategies. The key is to remember sustainable nutrition isn't supposed to take over your entire life; it should be one enjoyable part of it. Go out. Enjoy yourself. Plan ahead so you have some leeway. And if you do go over your calories, just get back on track the next day. You know how this goes by now.

How to Take the Anxiety Out of Going Out

The strategies we just shared are a great start for when you're eating out. But if you ever find yourself getting nervous, anxious, or worried before heading to a social event, read this section carefully, because we're going to give you tools to eliminate your nerves so you can relax and have fun.

Before we dive in, it's important to highlight the two main reasons why people trying to lose weight get anxious before going to a social event:

First: You don't want to ruin all of your progress. If you've been putting a ton of time and effort into your workouts and nutrition, the last thing you want to do is sabotage your results in a single night out.

Second: You don't know what food is going to be available and/or how many calories are in that food. This plays into the first fear of not wanting to ruin all of your progress, but it also speaks to a simple fear of the unknown. Anxiety stems from ambiguity. And when you don't have a plan (or the ability to plan, for that matter), it's much easier for anxiety to creep in.

With that in mind, here are a few strategies to help you stay on track while eating out, as well as reduce your anxiety about ruining all of your progress.

1. Remember, you can't fuck this up.

    It's critical to remember that the only way to fail is if you give up altogether. No one ever got skinny from eating one salad, just like no one ever got fat from eating one doughnut. Anytime you're worried about ruining all of your progress by going out to dinner with your friends and family, remind yourself of this, tell yourself to shut up, and go have fun.

2. Establish bright lines.

    A bright line is a steadfast rule you make for yourself that you cannot break. It isn't meant to be overly restrictive. It's simply meant to give you structure and a plan to follow. Because, remember, anxiety stems from ambiguity. So even if you don't know what food is going to be available or how many calories are in that food, you can create your own bright line(s) to help you stay on track and reduce your anxiety about the meal.

    For example, one of our personal favorite bright lines is the one-plate rule we recently mentioned. If you make that your rule for the night, you get one plate. Just one.

And you can have anything you like on it. But once that plate of food is finished, you're done eating.

You don't have to choose the one-plate rule as your bright line. There are many situations in which it might not make sense (e.g., a multicourse sit-down dinner). Just keep it in your back pocket as one potential bright line of many.

Another effective bright line we've used is the one-dessert rule. This is useful if you're at a celebration like Thanksgiving, for example, where there are often multiple desserts to choose from, each looking more delicious than the last. Instead of eating as much of every dessert as possible until you hate yourself and can't even stand up, pick one dessert and allow yourself to eat as much of that one dessert as you want. Research consistently shows this strategy leads to significantly fewer total calories eaten and also allows you to enjoy yourself rather than completely abstaining.

Bright lines are great for setting boundaries around alcohol, as well. Before going out, set a number of drinks that you're allowed to have, so there is no ambiguity when you get there. Maybe your bright line is a two-drink maximum. Maybe your bright line is to have at least one glass of water in between every alcoholic drink. There is no right or wrong here. The most important part of bright lines is that they are clear, specific, and once you decide to make them . . . you don't break them.

3. Use the "personal challenge" excuse.

This strategy works unbelievably well, especially if you happen to be in a group with someone obnoxious who keeps trying to get you to eat more, drink more, and do things you don't want to do. They usually say things like this:

Aww, come on, have another piece of cake! Live a little!

Don't be a Debbie Downer, get another drink!

We can't stand these kinds of people. But as obnoxious as they are, it's important to remember they're only trying to get you to eat more and drink more because they see you being so diligent, which in turn might make them feel bad about themselves. So, instead of getting their own habits in check, they try to manipulate your behavior to justify their own.

Regardless, this is where the "personal challenge" excuse works incredibly well. And, candidly, we're not sure why. But we've found when someone keeps obnoxiously trying to get you to indulge more, they immediately back off as soon as you tell them you're "doing a challenge," which is why you aren't eating/drinking more. You can say something like *I'm doing a 30-day no alcohol challenge* or *I'm doing a 14-day challenge where I don't eat dessert*. Honestly, it doesn't matter. You can make the challenge whatever you want it to be because it doesn't have to be real. The purpose is to get the obnoxious person off your back so you can enjoy yourself without someone being a pain in your ass. And, for whatever reason, telling people you're doing a challenge works like a charm.

How to Combat Sugar Cravings

Before we get into specific strategies, it's important for us to repeat ourselves for the fifty-seventh time and say there is no such thing as a "good" or "bad" food. And, with that in mind, sugar is not inherently bad for you. You can absolutely include sugar within your diet while improving your health, losing body fat, building muscle, and developing a better relationship with food. Some "fitness gurus" love to demonize sugar and blame it for all of the world's problems, but the fact of the matter is, sugar isn't the issue: too many calories is.

Not to mention, when most people say they're "addicted to sugar" and struggle with "uncontrollable sugar cravings," they don't realize sugar isn't the culprit. Think about it, if you were actually addicted to sugar, you'd keep a bag of Domino's pure sugar in your pantry at all times so you could slap a few spoonfuls back every time you needed a "hit." If it was purely a sugar problem, people would be uncontrollably eating some of the highest-sugar fruits like mangoes, grapes, and cherries. But no one is doing that. We've been led to believe sugar is the problem, when the truth is, it's synthetically designed foods with a combination of high-fat, high-sugar, and hyper-palatable traits driving these intense cravings.

Take, for example, doughnuts, cookies, and ice cream. Anti-sugar gurus label these as "bad" because they're high in sugar. But they're not purely sugar, are they? If they were, they wouldn't taste nearly as good, nor would they be so easy to keep eating without a second thought. The reason we crave them so much—and the reason they're so easy to overeat—is because of their high-fat, high-sugar combination. They are an example of what's known as hyper-palatable foods, and when it comes to overcoming your cravings, it's essential to understand what you're actually craving rather than demonizing a single ingredient.

Hyper-palatable foods aren't just high-fat and high-sugar. Take, for example, french fries. They have very little sugar, but they're an irresistible combination of high-fat and high-sodium. Some people struggle more with sweet cravings, whereas others struggle more with savory. Either way, sugar and salt alone are not the problem. And the sooner you understand this, the sooner you'll be able to gain control of your cravings.

With all of that out of the way, let's get to the crux of the issue: What can you do if you feel like you *need* a dessert every night and, no matter how hard you try, *you just can't stop*?

Many people liken their so-called sugar cravings to an addiction. Whether or not it's actually an addiction is a topic for another book. But, for the sake of discussion, what would you tell a friend who was struggling with alcohol addiction and said they feel like they *need* a drink every night and no matter how hard they try, they *just can't stop*?

Would you tell them it's not worth trying? Would you tell them they should give up and keep drinking because it's probably too hard to overcome? Of course not. They're your friend. You'd encourage them to believe that they *can* do it.

They can overcome their addiction. It's not going to be easy. It will be very difficult. But as long as they don't give up, they will succeed.

Back to you and your sugar cravings. Do you still think it's impossible to overcome? Do you think it's not worth trying simply because it's going to be difficult? Of course not. What an awful, defeatist mentality to live with. You can absolutely do this. There's no question about it. It won't be easy. There will be many challenging moments along the way. But if you take our advice, put it into practice, and fully commit to achieving your goals, there isn't a doubt in our minds that you can and will succeed.

So how can you overcome sugar cravings?

First, and this one can be annoying to hear, but it's important: you need to believe that you have control. Because you do. Whether you decide to eat something is completely and utterly in your control. And until you internalize this and take this responsibility unto yourself, you will continue to believe food has control over you instead of the other way around.

Second, and this one also sucks to hear, the best way to stop giving in to sugar cravings is to . . . stop giving in to them. You don't have to give up sugar entirely or forever. But if you consistently struggle with sugar cravings and have yet to find a balance, you must first go through a period of time in which you simply do not give in to them. It's easier said than done. We get that. But just because it's easier said than done doesn't mean it's not worth doing. And, for whatever it's worth, the first time saying "no" to the craving is by far the hardest. It's also the most important "no," because once you don't give in and instead prove to yourself that you have control over the food, you actually start to believe in your ability to succeed. And once you believe in yourself and understand that you have control over the food, you can start to incorporate it into your diet in moderation.

Third, instead of just saying "no" to whatever you're craving, replace it with something else you enjoy so you don't feel deprived. If you feel like you *absolutely, no exceptions, NEED* to have something sweet when a craving hits . . . well, remember that you don't. But regardless, you have many other delicious options to choose from, as well. Watermelon, strawberries, oranges, mangoes . . . there are so many options, and you can't go wrong with a bowl of fruit. You can also try Greek yogurt mixed with stevia to make it nice and sweet, then add in a scoop of your favorite protein powder and put it in the freezer for 10 minutes. It's quick, easy, filling, and tastes amazing. The options are endless, and you're only limited by your imagination. Just remember, *you* have control over the food, not the other way around.

Getting past sugar cravings can be one of the hardest things you go through as you try to lose weight and improve your health and relationship with food. But if you really do want to do it, you will push through the difficult times because you know it will be worth it on the other side. And, best of all, as time goes on and your relationship with food evolves, you *will* be able to eat sugar in moderation without it being all-or-nothing.

One Last Trick

Some people get a flood of anxiety when they get close to reaching their daily calorie limit. Their inner monologue becomes, *Oh crap, I'm almost out of calories. What do I do? How am I going to make it the rest of the day?* That fear can lead to a binge, which makes you think you've messed up. Which leads you down that road where you keep messing up because, well, you've already messed up.

We've already given you plenty of tools to help avoid that spiral. But here's one more hard-and-fast strategy you can use: set a bright line that allows you to add a specific number of calories to your day anytime you feel that anxiety building up. We usually recommend somewhere between 300 and 500 extra calories, but you can decide which amount would be best for you. When you do this, it helps silence the critic in your head that's trying to convince you you're screwing up. Those extra calories are allowed. They're part of your plan. And so is getting back on track tomorrow.

If you struggle with the fear and anxiety of running out of calories at the end of the day, this can be a huge help. Because if you don't create this rule and you just restrict, restrict, restrict, the anxiety builds up until you go ballistic and eat thousands upon thousands of extra calories. We would *much rather* you eat 500 extra calories one day and then get immediately back on track.

The hardest part of following this bright line is letting go of the fear that you're ruining all your progress by going over your calories. You know you aren't going to lose all your progress by eating a few hundred extra calories. And you also know it's better to go over by a few hundred extra calories than to restrict yourself until you uncontrollably binge and inhale an extra several thousand.

The point of this chapter is to be your toolbox. Just like you won't need every tool in your toolbox for every problem you have at home, you don't need to immediately use everything you found in this chapter. Use it as a reference and come back when you need a refresher. Use what works for you and discard what doesn't.

9

Creating Your Optimal Calorie Deficit for Fat Loss

This is it. This is what you've been waiting for. No more long, drawn-out explanations. No more chitchat or jibber jabber. In this chapter we're finally going to show you how to figure out the number of calories you should be eating to lose fat in a sustainable calorie deficit.

This chapter is going to be quick and to the point. We're going to outline our personal favorite calorie calculator so you can plug your numbers in and hit the ground running with a sustainable fat loss plan. With that said, there are two things worth briefly mentioning:

First, a quick Google search will reveal hundreds of differing calorie calculators. Each one will give you slightly different numbers and they'll all claim to be "the best" and "most accurate." Obviously, that's nonsense because our calculator is the best and most accurate. Kidding. But, seriously, joking aside, we do think ours is the best or else we wouldn't use it. But, frankly, just pick one and use it. Your numbers don't need to be "perfect," and there is no such thing as a one-size-fits-all calorie calculator. The most important thing you can do is just pick one and get to work following it consistently.

Second, as we mentioned in the previous chapter, odds are you're going to think the calories we've given you are too high. They are not. If you've lost weight in the past by starving yourself only to gain it all back a short while later, clearly what you did was unsustainable. The calories you'll receive from our calculation will be higher, but, we promise, they do put you in a calorie deficit so you will lose fat. They'll also allow you to enjoy your favorite foods in moderation while losing fat so that the process is significantly more sustainable and enjoyable. So, before you email us asking if we think your calories are too high, delete the draft and reread this paragraph.

Without further ado, let's figure out your calorie deficit.

Calculating Your Calories

Step 1

Multiply your goal body weight by 12. For example, if your goal body weight is 175 pounds, 175 × 12 = 2,100. This means you could eat 2,100 calories/day and lose fat in a sustainable calorie deficit.

A couple things to keep in mind regarding your goal body weight:

- **Don't overthink it:** You can pick a weight that you think would be your absolute leanest. Or you can choose more of an intermediary goal weight somewhere along the way. For example, if you're currently 300 pounds and your ultimate goal body weight is 175 pounds, you can either go straight to 175 × 12 (2,100 calories/day) or begin with something a little less extreme, like 225 × 12 (which would allot you 2,700 calories/day). Both work very well and neither is inherently better or worse than the other. Choosing your ultimate goal weight would obviously lead to faster progress, but remember, faster isn't always better. Choose whichever you think will be best for you long term.

- **Don't get attached to it:** There is zero reason to get emotionally attached to your goal body weight. You don't need to weigh that exact amount to achieve your ultimate goal. If your goal body weight is 175 pounds and you love how you look and feel when you get to 190 pounds, cool, you're done. You aren't required to get to 175 simply because you used that as your multiplier. All you need to do is pick a weight lighter than you currently are and use that to determine how many calories you should be eating. The lower your goal weight, the lower your calories will be.

Step 2

Establish an appropriate caloric range. If you set your goal weight at 175 pounds, your daily caloric intake would be 2,100 calories. That said, and as we spoke about previously, it's better to establish a range of calories rather than try to hit an exact number. With that in mind, a range of +/–100 calories on either end is sufficient. So, using the example from above, instead of trying to hit precisely 2,100 calories, your daily caloric range would be between 2,000 and 2,200 calories.

Step 3

Be consistent and track your progress for at least 30 days. Most people who hit these calories consistently (80 percent consistent would be at least 24 days in a month) will lose between 1 and 3 percent of their total body weight. For a 200-pound person, that would be between 2 and 6 pounds lost over that month. If you fall within that range, perfect, keep going. You've found a sustainable calorie deficit. If you've lost less than 1 percent of your total body weight, you can slightly decrease your calorie range. And if you've lost more than 3 percent of your total body weight, you can slightly increase your calorie range. However, it's important for you to be honest with your level of consistency. If you've only been 50 percent consistent, you're obviously not going to see the progress you want. In that case, your priority should be to increase consistency before changing your calories.

(Optional) Step 4

If you follow the instructions above, you will have everything you need to lose weight sustainably and enjoyably. But if you want us to do the calculations for you, simply download Mike's free app, Mike's Macros. No, this isn't a sales pitch, and there's no catch. It's 100 percent free with no ads. Just plug your data in, and we'll tell you exactly what your calories and macros should be.

Calculating Your Protein

Now that you've got your calories figured out, it's time to get your protein sorted.

Step 1

Multiply your goal body weight by 1. For example, if your goal body weight is 175 pounds, 175 × 1 = 175. This means you would eat a minimum of 175 grams of protein per day.

A couple things to keep in mind regarding your protein intake:

- **This target is a minimum:** Using the example from above, 175 grams of protein per day would be your *minimum* target. You are welcome to eat more than that if you so choose. That said, as long as you hit this minimum amount, you are not required to eat more.
- **It gets easier the more you do it:** Many people struggle to hit their protein when they first start making these lifestyle changes. That's normal, so you shouldn't quit because it's difficult. Keep going. We guarantee that as you consistently eat more protein, you'll notice your

hunger and weight going down while your strength and muscle definition improve.

(Optional) Calculating Your Carbs and Fats

Once you've calculated your daily calorie and protein targets, you're good to go. You don't need to track your carbs and fat to lose weight. Jordan prefers doing exactly this, simply sticking to his calories and protein. Mike, on the other hand, prefers tracking all of his macronutrients (proteins, carbs, and fats). Both methods work; it just depends on what you prefer.

With that in mind, if you'd like us to calculate all of your macros for you, including carbs and fats, download Mike's free app, Mike's Macros, from the App Store. Again, it's free and there's no catch, so if you'd like to have all of your macros calculated for you, just download Mike's Macros and you'll be good to go.

To Recap...

Using the example from above, if your goal weight is 175 pounds, this is how you would calculate your total daily calorie and protein intake.

Step 1: Calories

$175 \times 12 = 2{,}100$ calories/day

Step 2: Your calorie range

+/–100 = a range of 2,000 to 2,200 calories/day

Step 3: Protein

175 × 1 = 175 grams of protein/day (minimum)

That's it. You're good to go. It might seem "too simple," but, we promise, if you consistently hit these calorie and protein guidelines, you will lose fat slowly and sustainably while having the freedom to enjoy your favorite foods.

With all that said, now that you have your mindset and nutrition taken care of, it's time to talk about another essential aspect of health and fitness: lifting weights and getting stronger.

Part III
Lift It!

10

Strength Training

Here's the truth: if your goal is solely weight loss, you don't *need* to exercise. We're probably going to get some angry emails about this one. But, as you already know, in order to lose fat, you simply need to be in a calorie deficit. That being said, just because you don't *need* to do something doesn't mean you shouldn't do it. Not to mention, we doubt your goal is to lose weight without improving your strength or health. Because if you want to get healthier, stronger, and have more muscle definition . . . exercise *is* essential.

The question is . . . what type of exercise? If your primary goal is fat loss and close secondary goals are to get stronger, more defined, more athletic, and feel/move better, what kind of exercise should you be focusing on? High-intensity interval training (HIIT)? Hot yoga? Tabata? Orangetheory? Peloton? Should you start training for a marathon? Jazzercise? Shake Weight? Cardio kickboxing? Pilates? Barry's Bootcamp? We could go on like this for several more pages, but we'll spare you the nonsense.

The options are endless. And every half-assed personal trainer on Instagram will swear up and down *their* method is *the best* way to exercise for fat loss. The truth is, strength training is, without question, the best form of exercise for fat loss. We guarantee this will get us some 1-star reviews on Amazon, but if your goal is to lose fat and keep it off forever, strength training needs to be your priority.

We are not saying all other forms of exercise are useless. Nor are we saying they can't (or don't) improve your health. Any exercise is better than none at all. And just because strength training is optimal for fat loss, that doesn't mean cardio or other types of exercise should be excluded from your workout regimen. In fact, that couldn't be farther from the truth. Cardio can (and should) be a regular part of your exercise routine, but it should be done to improve your health, *not* to burn as many calories as possible for fat loss.

We need to emphasize this point because when most people want to lose fat, the first thing they try is the treadmill, StairMaster, or cardio kickboxing class at the Y. They think the only way they'll be able to lose fat is if they do hours of cardio, get drenched in sweat, crank their heart rate up, and burn as many calories as they possibly can. While there's nothing wrong with doing cardio (again, you should do it to improve your health), you do not need to do hours of it to lose fat. In fact, from a fat loss perspective, you would be better off spending less time on the treadmill and more time lifting heavy weights.

Why Strength Training Is Best for Fat Loss

First things first: if you're scared to lift heavy weights because you think you're going to get "too bulky" and look like a bodybuilder, shut up. In the nicest way possible and said with all of our love, shut up. To borrow our earlier analogy, not lifting heavy weights because you don't want to look like a bodybuilder is like not driving a car because you don't want to become a NASCAR driver. Building muscle takes time. A lot of time. And a tremendous amount of patience and effort. You're not going to accidentally get too big or bulky, we promise.

Not to mention, if you want to get more "toned" and have some muscle definition, that's not going to come from yoga or Pilates or Friday-morning Zumba class. Those are great forms of exercise, and if you love them, do them. But if you want to get toned with real muscle definition . . . *you need to build muscle.* And the only way to build muscle is through strength training, lifting progressively heavier weights and challenging yourself to get stronger over time.

Having said all of that, here are several other reasons why strength training is the best form of exercise for fat loss and a better quality of life:

- **More Muscle = Faster Metabolism:** The more muscle you have, the more calories your body will burn throughout the day (even when you sleep). So, while cardio may burn a few hundred calories in a single workout, strength training and building muscle allows you to burn more calories all day, every day. Which allows you to eat *more* food while continuing to lose fat. This is especially important for the women who are worried their metabolism has slowed down as they've gotten older; lifting weights will substantially increase your metabolism.

- **Better Results in Less Time:** Most people think you need to work out for 1–2 hours/day, 6–7 days/week to get great results. You don't. If you're strength training properly and following a well-designed workout (as we give you in the following chapters), you will get incredible results with 45-to-60-minute workouts, 3–4 days/week. Because what most don't realize is that your body will only get stronger and build muscle if you give it time to rest and recover. So, while working out is obviously important, taking adequate rest is equally important if you actually want to see your body change.

- **Reduced Risk of Injury:** Injury prevention is a topic that could fill a library on its own, so we won't try to explain it all in this brief paragraph. It is important to know, however, proper strength training doesn't just help you get stronger and more defined, it also makes your body more resilient and less likely to get injured. Not to mention, strength training has proven to reduce and eliminate chronic pain time and again. So, whether your goal is fat loss or not, strength training is essential for the overall improvement of your health and well-being.

- **Solves the "Skinny Fat" Problem:** Over the years we've worked with thousands of people who don't just want to lose weight . . . they also want to get stronger and more defined. They work out, but they tell us they don't look like they work out and they aren't sure how to fix it. The answer: strength training. You can take your HIIT classes and ride your spin bike all day long, but if you don't lift some damn weights, you're still gonna have noodle arms and a pancake butt.

• **Increased Bone Density:** Everyone talks about wanting to increase their metabolism, but they completely overlook the importance of increasing their bone density. One of the main causes of death as people (especially women) get older is falling and breaking their hip. Again, cardio is wonderful, but all the cardio in the world will do nothing for improving your bone density. Arguably the best thing you can do to "bulletproof" your body as you get older is lift weights and strength train, which results in increased bone density.

• **Longer Life Span:** Studies show that both men and women who strength train are at a lower risk of all-cause mortality (i.e., death). One study found that doing up to 145 minutes (less than 2.5 hours) of strength training per week led to increased longevity in older women, even if they did zero cardio.[*]

If you want to get stronger, have more muscle definition, ramp up your metabolism, improve your health, and increase

[*] Masamitsu Kamada et al., "Strength Training and All-Cause, Cardiovascular Disease, and Cancer Mortality in Older Women: A Cohort Study," *Journal of the American Heart Association*, John Wiley and Sons Inc., October 31, 2017, https://www.ncbi.nlm.nih.gov/pmc/articles/PMC5721806/.

the resiliency of your body . . . strength training is essential. You don't need to be in the gym for 2 hours/day, 7 days/week. You don't need to worry about looking like a juiced-up bodybuilder. And you don't need to have an outrageously expensive gym membership or any fancy equipment. If you follow our guidelines and the strength training workouts in the coming chapters, you'll see you can reap all the benefits of strength training in just a few hours per week.

Strength Training Essentials

To get the most out of your strength training, you need to follow each of these six essentials.

1. Full-Body, Compound Exercises

There's nothing wrong with biceps curls or triceps extensions (we'll include both within your workouts). But these small isolation exercises that only hit a single muscle group shouldn't make up the majority of your workout. Rather, you want to emphasize full-body, compound exercises that target several large muscle groups with each and every repetition. They recruit significantly more muscle fiber than isolation exercises, they carry over to real life better, and they give you infinitely more bang for your buck in that they get you in and out of the gym in a fraction of the time.

Squats, deadlifts, lunges, and hip thrusts are examples of great lower body exercises that hit numerous large muscle groups all at once. Bench presses, chin-ups, rows, and shoulder presses are great for the upper body.

For the best results, the first few exercises of each workout should be heavy, full-body, compound exercises. And the last few exercises can be smaller, isolation exercises to bring up individual muscle groups. You'll see exactly how we structure this in Chapters 12 and 13.

2. Adequate Rest Between Sets

Many people speed through their workouts as fast as they can, taking as little rest as possible because they think sweating more and cranking their heart rate up is the key to a good workout. These are also the same people who are never happy with their results and can't figure out why, no matter how hard they go in the gym, they never see the progress they want.

Remember, sweat is not a valid indicator of an effective workout. It's not bad if you sweat, but if your workout priority is to sweat as much as possible, you're missing the forest for the trees and will never actually look like you lift. Getting stronger and building muscle will do more for your performance and physique than sweating ever will. And, in order to get stronger, you need to give your body sufficient rest so you can recover.

When you're emphasizing heavy, full-body, compound exercises, you need to prioritize rest between sets. Generally speaking, 2–4 minutes of complete rest in between heavy sets is optimal. At the beginning of your workout (when you're lifting the heaviest weights), your rest periods should be closer to 4 minutes. As you make your way through the workout, you can progressively reduce it until you get 2 minutes of rest between sets. Then, when you get to the isolation exercises, you can limit rest to 60–75 seconds between sets. No need to memorize this, though, because we'll outline it for you in your workouts in the coming chapters.

3. Good Technique

This should go without saying, but we have to say it: using proper technique is more important than lifting heavier weight. Not only because it's going to keep you safe and reduce the risk of injury but also because proper technique ensures you're actually training the right muscle groups. If you want to get stronger and more defined but you regularly sacrifice technique to put more weight on the bar, you are never going to get the results you want . . . and you're probably going to end up at a physical therapist's office, healing a snapped spine. Kidding. But seriously.

If you aren't sure how to do an exercise safely, we've prepared an extensive exercise database for you here: www.youtube.com/eatitworkout. If the exercise you want isn't there, you can join Jordan's Inner Circle (www.sfinnercircle.com), where he has hundreds of exercise video tutorials. Or just type the exercise name into the Google machine and you'll find countless video tutorials for free.

4. Consistency Is King

You know this by now. Just like nobody ever got fat from eating one burger or skinny from eating one salad—you won't get stronger or visible muscle definition by lifting occasionally. And you won't lose all of your progress if you happen to skip one or two workouts. If you can be 80 percent consistent (for years) with your workouts, you will make incredible progress.

Worth mentioning is **the Rule of 5**. Originally written by world-renowned strength coach and lecturer Dan John, the Rule of 5 is an important concept to keep in mind when you're struggling to stay consistent with your workouts. The Rule of 5 says, for every 5 workouts you will have:

- 1 incredible workout
- 1 awful workout
- And 3 average, nothing-to-write-home-about workouts

The Rule of 5 is helpful because most people give up and quit when they feel like they've stopped making progress. When they have a couple of "meh" workouts and irrationally conclude the workouts are no longer working. Don't make this mistake. Every workout isn't going to be your best. And the stronger you get over time, the harder your workouts are going to become. Be patient. Stay consistent. And remember that showing up is 90 percent of the battle.

5. Progressive Overload

Arguably the most important of all, progressive overload is just a fancy way of saying, "Put your body under more stress over time." Keep in mind, stress (in this sense) is actually a good thing. Lifting weights is, technically, a stressor on your body that, as you rest, allows your body to recover and become stronger than it was prior to that stressor. The most popular (and fun) way to incorporate progressive overload is by lifting heavier weight. It doesn't need to be a lot. Even adding 2.5 pounds is enough to elicit a response. But, unfortunately, you won't be able to lift heavier every single day, week, or even every month. So, as you get stronger and become a more advanced lifter, you will need to find other ways to progressively overload your body so you can continue to build strength, grow muscle, and improve your performance. Other ways to incorporate progressive overload are:

- Do more repetitions with the same weight
- Use better technique (or a bigger range of motion) with the same weight
- Slightly reduce the rest period (even by 5–10 seconds) while lifting the same weight
- Do more total sets with the same weight
- Increase time under tension (emphasized eccentrics, static holds, 1.5 reps, etc.)

The biggest mistake most new lifters make with progressive overload is thinking they need to (or should be able to) lift heavier weight every time they work out. This will not happen. Think about it like this: if you add a measly 5 pounds to your bench press every week, that would be +260 pounds in a year, +520 pounds in 2 years. Most lifters never bench press anywhere near that much in their entire career, never mind within 2 years. And this is only an increase of 5 pounds per week. Keep this in mind as you go to the gym and challenge yourself to get stronger. There are many ways to incorporate progressive overload, and even teeny tiny, seemingly insignificant improvements make a huge difference over time.

6. Rest Days

We'll get straight to the point: lifting weights every day is stupid. Some people think you need to lift every day to optimize your progress, and we strongly urge you to never take advice from these people ever again because they have no clue what they're talking about. Lifting weights every single day will hurt, not help you. If you're lifting weights properly, you're putting your muscles, tendons, ligaments, joints, and even nervous system under a significant amount of stress. Rest days give your body the opportunity to recover and come back stronger than it was before, whereas lifting every day suppresses your body's ability to recover and does more harm than good over time. In the workouts we've written for you, you will be lifting 3–4 days/week. Do not add more. Take the rest days as we've programmed. If you don't, you will not make the progress you want.

Client Spotlight

More Is Not Better. Better Is Better.

"I've been a personal trainer for over six years. When I started, I worked out six days a week because I thought that was the only way I could make progress on my fitness goals. I began working with Jordan because I wanted someone to help design my workouts, and the biggest change he had me make was scaling back to only working out four days a week. It was a huge transition. And it was scary. But I didn't realize just how unmotivated and lethargic I'd become because I was pushing myself to work out too much. I was worried I'd gain fat if I didn't move enough, or that I'd lose any progress I made, even though my body was telling me I needed to rest.

"What I wasn't expecting, though, was the mental shift. It made me more honest and transparent with myself. Once I started to really believe I couldn't fuck this up, I was able to trust the process more. I used to be very aesthetically goal-oriented. But once I made that mental shift I even started going to therapy. I realized that until I learned to work on the inside out, then I will never be satisfied with any physical goals or progress that I make."

—Ryan

"When I came to Jordan, I was an over-exerciser. I worked out six, sometimes seven days a week. Sometimes twice in the day. And I told everybody, 'I love it. This is what I want to do.' And there is truth to that. I did love it, but I didn't realize I was also driven by fear. I worked out compulsively because I was afraid if I didn't, I was going to gain fat; I was not going to make progress; or I was going to lose whatever progress I had made.

"The irony is, I was making no progress. Then, when I scaled back to working out four days a week, my progress increased exponentially.

"It just comes down to letting your body recover. When you

do that, your next workout is going to be better than it would have been. I still have people who are amazed that I only work out four days a week. But that works beautifully. And it is such a big lesson I've learned: More is not better. Better is better."

—*Susan*

Strength Training FAQ

Before you dive into your workouts, we want to take a moment to answer some frequently asked questions about strength training. Make sure you read this section in its entirety before trying the workouts, because it's going to help you understand where to begin and how to progress moving forward.

How many times per week should I strength train?

Minimum: 2×/week (full-body workouts)
Maximum: 5×/week (body part split)
Optimal (for most people): 3–4×/week (upper body/lower body split)

The workout programs we've written for you in the following chapters are 3–4×/week because, for the vast majority of people, this frequency provides the best results in the least amount of time. If you can only strength train 2×/week, that's fine but not optimal. And in this scenario we'd recommend doing two full-body workouts each week. If you prefer to strength train 5×/week, that's okay, but it's important to understand it is not inherently better than 3–4×/week, and in that scenario you'd be better off following a body part split.

How long should each workout take?

If you follow the workouts we've written for you, each one will last somewhere between 45 and 75 minutes (depending on how much you're texting during the workout). If you're finishing the workouts in less than 45 minutes, odds are you aren't lifting heavy enough. If the workouts take you longer than 75 minutes, stop scrolling through Instagram and get to work.

Do I need to do a warm-up before working out?

Yes, you need to do a warm-up before working out, and we'll give you one to follow in the workout chapters. The purpose of your warm-up is to increase your body temperature, improve your range of motion, get your joints moving more freely, and help prevent injury. With that said, your warm-up should be no longer than 10–15 minutes at an absolute maximum. Most people walk on the treadmill for 20 seconds and follow that up with a few arm swings and an off-balanced quad stretch before jumping right into their workout. Don't be most people. Follow the warm-up in the workout chapters.

How do I know how much weight to start with?

If you've never done an exercise before and you aren't sure which weight to begin with, remember this rule of thumb: you would rather start too light than too heavy. In some instances (like with a squat) this could mean beginning with just your body weight. In other cases (like with a dumbbell bench press), it might be a pair of 20-pound dumbbells. Either way, if you aren't sure where to start, always err on the side of caution.

How do I know when to increase the weight?

Generally speaking, the last 2–4 repetitions of your work sets should be *very* difficult. If you're finishing your set without much difficulty, increase the weight by 5–10 pounds. That being said, you should still be able to finish the set with good technique. So, if you can't complete all of the prescribed repetitions with solid form, you need to drop the weight by at least 5–10 pounds.

For example, let's say you're doing dumbbell bench press for 3 × 10 (3 sets of 10 reps) with 25 pounds in each hand. If you can do all 10 repetitions without much of a struggle, increase the weight to 30 pounds in each hand. If you complete all 10 reps but the last few reps are very challenging, keep the weight the same. And if you can't complete all 10 reps with good technique, reduce the weight to 20 pounds per hand.

Do I need to do a cool-down?

No, you don't need to do a cool-down. Candidly, the two of us have been training for a combined thirty-eight years, and we are not exaggerating when we say neither of us have *ever*, in our *entire lives*, done a cool-down after a workout. If you want to do one, go for it. But it is in no way, shape, or form essential.

What about cardio?

You'll notice we don't include cardio in our workout programs. That's because you don't need it to lose fat and build muscle. That said, cardio is immensely important for your overall health (physical and mental), and we strongly urge you to make it a regular part of your weekly exercise routine. The great part about cardio is it's far less complicated than strength training. You don't need to worry about sets and reps. You don't need to meticulously scrutinize your technique. And you don't need to have access to any fancy equipment. Go on a walk or a jog or a run. Swim in a pool or a lake or the ocean. Take a bike ride. Hop on the elliptical. Do a dance class. Try jiujitsu. Just get your body moving. Ideally, aim for at least 150 minutes (2½ hours) of cardiovascular exercise every week. But if you can do more, amazing, because that will be incredible for your health. If you want to keep it as simple as possible, try to get 7,000–10,000 steps/day. If you can do that on a regular basis, your health will radically improve.

Should I do weights or cardio first?

Unless you're an elite athlete, it doesn't really make a difference. Ideally, you would do them on separate days and save your cardiovascular exercise (walking, swimming, jogging, cycling, etc.) for your non-lifting days. If your schedule doesn't allow you to do that, however, we recommend doing your strength training before your cardio. You want to be as fresh and focused as possible for your weight training so you can lift heavy without risking injury.

How many calories should I aim to burn from strength training?

Trick question. You shouldn't be trying to track how many calories you burn from exercise regardless of whether it's strength training or cardio. Aside from the fact that the popular mainstream tools people use to track calories burned are wrong by upward of 50 percent, the purpose of your workout is *not* to burn as many calories as possible. The purpose is to get stronger, increase your endurance, improve your mobility, and reach other markers of performance that actually make a difference in your life. The more you focus on calories burned, the more you're missing the forest for the trees.

Should I eat back the calories I burned during exercise?

No. First and foremost, you shouldn't even be tracking your calories burned, for the reasons we just outlined. Not to mention, since the calorie tracker you're using is wildly inaccurate, you don't actually know how many calories you're burning from exercise. Unless you're an elite endurance athlete exercising for hours on end every single day, do not think about the calories you burn during exercise. They do not matter in terms of your performance, progress, or programming. If you're wondering how you're supposed to know your calorie deficit if you don't know how many calories you're burning, refer back to Chapter 9 and follow the calorie deficit calculation we provided you.

Free weights or machines?

You'll notice the workouts we've written for you are all free weights, no machines. This is not because machines are bad. They aren't. Machines are a great tool, they have many benefits, and we use them regularly for ourselves and our clients. That said, free weights tend to carry over better into your everyday life. Not to mention, not everyone has access to the same machines. So we decided to write your programs utilizing free weights because they are more readily accessible to the masses (not to mention far less expensive). Keep in mind, utilizing both free weights and machines is probably better than either alone, so we encourage you to use both as you progress in your training career.

Should I feel sore after I lift weights?

We'll put it like this: if you're never sore after lifting weights, you're not lifting heavy enough. On the other hand, if you're always debilitatingly sore after lifting weights, you're lifting too heavy (and probably with terrible technique). Soreness is not a valid indicator of whether your workout was effective. But it is a common side effect of effective workouts. So, yes, you can and should expect to feel sore after strength training. But if there are times in which you aren't sore, don't worry, that isn't a bad sign. Some days you'll be more sore than others, and that's completely normal. It's worth mentioning that if you're brand-new to lifting weights, you are probably going to be *very* sore—far more sore than you'll be once your body has adapted to these workouts.

Do I need to train my abs?

Yes, of course. Your abdominals are muscles, and, just like every other muscle group in your body, you need to train them for them to get stronger. That said, it's important to understand that training your abs will *not* make your abs more visible. Just because you do ab exercises doesn't mean you're going to get a six-pack. The only way to make your abs more visible is to lose enough body fat (via a calorie deficit) to the point where your ab muscles begin to show. Also worth mentioning, some coaches (including us in the past) say the only ab exercises you need are big compound lifts like squats and deadlifts. They are wrong. To optimize your core training, you need to train your abs with varying weights, intensities, and movement patterns. You don't need to do anything crazy, and you don't need an entire day just for your abs, but it is important to have specific exercises dedicated solely to core strength.

What's the best time of day to lift weights?

It doesn't matter. Seriously. Work out when you can fit it into your schedule. If that is in the morning before work, great. If that is in the afternoon around lunch, great. If that is in the evening after work, great. Just make sure you work out and schedule it in a way that allows you to do it consistently.

11

Before We Start Lifting

If you're a seasoned gym rat and feel confident diving right into the strength training program, feel free to skip this chapter. If you would like a little more guidance on how to read, adjust, and apply the workouts, that's what we're going to cover right now. Some of what we say might seem obvious, but we want to cover all of our bases and make sure you feel confident and ready walking into your first training session.

Your Gym Bag

First things first, before you even step foot in the gym, let's make sure you have everything you need in your gym bag. A water bottle and clean face towel are always a good idea to have on hand. If you want to reduce the chances of someone talking to you during your workout, make sure you have a pair of headphones to slap on and keep the creepers at bay. As for footwear, comfort is the primary importance, but for strength training specifically it's important to have a shoe with a hard, flat sole (i.e., not a running shoe). Reason being, running shoes have a cushioned sole and are designed to absorb force. This is great for reducing the impact on your joints when you run. For strength training, however, it reduces your ability to put force directly into the ground and can even make you slightly unbalanced due to the curvature of the sole. With that in mind, we recommend any shoe you feel comfortable in with a hard, flat sole (Converse All Stars, New Balance Minimus, etc.).

Your Workout Frequency

Following our programs you can choose between working out 3 or 4 times each week. Please, do not overcomplicate or overthink this decision. If you are incredibly busy and/or don't like working out very often, choose the 3×/week option. If you have more time on your hands and/or prefer working out more frequently, choose the 4×/week option. They are both equally effective so long as you are consistent in doing them.

Your Exercise Technique

As we mentioned earlier, if you aren't sure what an exercise is or how to do it properly, you can use our exercise database here: www.youtube.com/eatitworkout.

Your Sets and Reps

Next to each exercise you'll see how many sets and repetitions of that exercise you're supposed to do.

For example: *Barbell Deadlift: 3 × 5*

The first number (3) is the total number of sets you're going to perform. And the second number (5) is the total number of repetitions you're going to do per set. So, for this example, you would do Barbell Deadlifts for 3 sets of 5 reps. Between each set you'll take a full rest (as we outlined in our strength training essentials) before moving on to the next set. Once all 3 sets are completed, you will progress to the next exercise.

Your Workout Order of Events

As you review your workout, you'll notice the exercises are grouped and labeled by a corresponding number and letter (1a, 1b, 2a, 2b, 2c, etc.). The numbers simply denote the order in which you will perform the exercises. So, for example, 1 is the first exercise of the day, 2 is the second exercise, and so on. The letters next to each number represent what is known as either a "superset" or "circuit." A super-set is when you alternate between two exercises, and a circuit is when you cycle through three (or more) exercises in a row.

To illustrate, we'll walk you through a sample lower body workout:

1a) Barbell Deadlift: 3 × 5

2a) Dumbbell Front Squat: 3 × 8

2b) Long Lever Hollow Body Hold: 3 × 20sec

3a) Single-Leg Romanian Deadlift: 3 × 10/leg

3b) Glute Bridge: 3 × 10

3c) Side Plank: 3 × 15sec/side

The first exercise (1a) is a Barbell Deadlift. It is not paired with another exercise, so after completing 3 sets of 5 reps you will progress to the second exercise.

The second exercise grouping (2a) is Dumbbell Front Squat and it is paired (2b) with Long Lever Hollow Body Hold. This is a superset, and you will alternate between these two exercises until you have completed 3 sets of each exercise.

The third exercise grouping is a circuit of (3a) Single-Leg Romanian Deadlift, (3b) Glute Bridge, and (3c) Side Plank. You will cycle through these three exercises in a circuit fashion until you have completed 3 sets of each exercise.

Why Separate Workouts for Men and Women?

For the record, you can choose to do any of the workouts in this book regardless of your gender. They're all full-body workouts, and you'll get amazing results if you do them consistently.

The only difference between our workouts for men and women is the body parts that are emphasized. The general trend we've noticed, through years of training hundreds of thousands of folks, is that men often want to emphasize toning up their chest, arms, and shoulders. And the general trend we've noticed for women is that they often want to emphasize toning their back, shoulders, and glutes. So each program is designed accordingly.

But again: anyone who does either program will get a full-body workout. It's just a matter of which zones you want to emphasize.

With all that said, you're ready to begin. You're fully prepared and equipped with everything you need to know to improve your mindset, understand nutrition, and start strength training. Even if you don't feel ready, we promise you have everything you need to start. We're not saying it's going to be an easy journey. But it will be worth it. And as long as you don't quit, you will get stronger and more confident and love the way you look.

12

Workouts for Men

Warm-Up

1. Brisk Walk: 5 minutes
2. Calf Stretch: 20 seconds per leg
3. Kneeling Hip Flexor Stretch: 20 seconds per leg
4. Split Stance Adductor Mobilization: 10 per leg
5. T-Spine Extension/Rotation: 10/side
6. Glute Bridge: 10
7. Band Pull-Apart: 10

Four Days/Week Workout Program

Mon / Wed / Fri / Sat

Day 1: Lower Body, Abs, Arms
1a) Barbell Deadlift: 3 × 5

2a) Dumbbell Loaded Front Squat: 3 × 8
2b) Long Lever Hollow Body Hold: 3 × 20sec

3a) Single-Leg Romanian Deadlift: 3 × 10/leg
3b) Side Plank: 3 × 15sec/side

4a) Standing Overhand Grip EZ Bar Curl: 3 × 8
4b) Standing Underhand Grip EZ Bar Curl: 3 × 12

Day 2: Upper Body
1a) Chin-Up (weighted or assisted as needed): 3 × 6

2a) Seated Dumbbell Shoulder Press: 3 × 8

3a) Single-Arm Dumbbell Row: 3 × 10/arm
3b) Single-Arm Flat Dumbbell Bench Press: 3 × 10/arm

4a) Kneeling Single-Arm Lat Pulldown: 3 × 12/arm
4b) Single-Arm Leaning Lateral Shoulder Raise with Cable:
    3 × 15/arm
4c) Face Pull: 3 × 12

5a) Chest Supported Dumbbell Spider Curl: 2 × 20
5b) Standing Dumbbell Overhead Triceps Extension: 2 × 15

Day 3: Lower Body and Abs

1a) Barbell Back Squat: 3 × 6

2a) Dumbbell Lateral Lunge with Goblet Hold: 3 × 8/leg

3a) Hanging Knee Raise: 3 × 12
3b) Single-Leg Hip Thrust: 3 × 12/leg

4a) Russian Twist: 3 × 12/side

Day 4: Upper Body

1a) Flat Barbell Bench Press: 3 × 8

2a) Bent Over Barbell Row: 4 × 8

3a) Seated Alternating Dumbbell Hammer Curl: 3 × 6/arm
3b) Seated Bent Over Dumbbell Rear Delt Fly: 3 × 12

4a) Feet Inclined Push-Up: 3 × 12

5a) Chest Supported Row: 3 × 15
5b) Farmer's Carry: 3 × 30sec

Three Days/Week Workout Program

Mon / Tues / Fri

Day 1: Upper Body
1a) Chin-Up (weighted or assisted as needed): 3 × 6

2a) Seated Dumbbell Shoulder Press: 3 × 8

3a) Single-Arm Dumbbell Row: 3 × 10/arm
3b) Single-Arm Flat Dumbbell Bench Press: 3 × 10/arm

4a) Kneeling Single-Arm Lat Pulldown: 3 × 12/arm
4b) Single-Arm Leaning Lateral Shoulder Raise with Cable:
      3 × 15/arm
4c) Face Pull: 3 × 12

5a) Chest Supported Dumbbell Spider Curl: 2 × 20
5b) Standing Dumbbell Overhead Triceps Extension: 2 × 15

Day 2: Lower Body and Abs
1a) Barbell Back Squat: 3 × 5

2a) Dumbbell Lateral Lunge with Goblet Hold: 3 × 6/leg
2b) Long Lever Hollow Body Hold: 3 × 20sec

3a) Cable Pull Thru: 3 × 10
3b) Cable Crunch: 3 × 10

4a) Single-Leg Hip Thrust: 3 × 10/leg
4b) Russian Twist: 3 × 10/side

Day 3: Upper Body

1a) Flat Barbell Bench Press: 3 × 8

2a) Bent Over Barbell Row: 4 × 8

3a) Seated Alternating Dumbbell Hammer Curl: 3 × 6/arm
3b) Seated Bent Over Dumbbell Rear Delt Fly: 3 × 12

4a) Feet Inclined Push-Up: 3 × 12

5a) Chest Supported Row: 3 × 15
5b) Farmer's Carry: 3 × 30sec

13

Workouts for Women

Warm-Up

1. Brisk Walk: 5 minutes
2. Calf Stretch: 20 seconds per leg
3. Kneeling Hip Flexor Stretch: 20 seconds per leg
4. Split Stance Adductor Mobilization: 10 per leg
5. T-Spine Extension/Rotation: 10/side
6. Glute Bridge: 10
7. Band Pull-Apart: 10

Four Days/Week Workout Program

Mon / Wed / Fri / Sat

Day 1: Lower Body and Abs
1a) Sumo Deadlift: 3 × 5
1b) Glute Bridge: 3 × 10

2a) Goblet Squat: 3 × 10
2b) Dumbbell Romanian Deadlift: 3 × 10
2c) Single-Leg Plank: 3 × 15sec/leg

3a) Dumbbell Reverse Lunge: 3 × 12/leg
3b) Leg Curl on Physio Ball: 3 × 12
3c) Bicycle Crunch: 3 × 12/side

Day 2: Upper Body
1a) Dumbbell Bench Press: 3 × 8
1b) Dumbbell Row: 3 × 8/arm

2a) Push-Up: 3 × 10 (elevate your hands if needed)
2b) Batwing Row: 3 × 12
2c) Dumbbell Front Shoulder Raise: 3 × 12

3a) Seated Dumbbell Shoulder Press: 3 × 12
3b) Seated Dumbbell Hammer Curl: 3 × 12/arm
3c) Seated Dumbbell Overhead Triceps Extension: 3 × 12

Day 3: Lower Body and Abs

1a) Squat: 3 × 6
1b) Side Plank: 3 × 12sec/side

2a) Single-Leg Romanian Deadlift: 3 × 8/leg
2b) Bulgarian Split Squat: 3 × 8/leg
2c) Long Lever Plank: 3 × 20sec

3a) Single-Leg Hip Thrust: 3 × 15/leg
3b) Close Stance Goblet Squat: 3 × 15
3c) Russian Twist: 3 × 12/side

Day 4: Upper Body

1a) Seated Alternating Dumbbell Shoulder Press: 3 × 10/arm
1b) Dumbbell Row w/ Pause at Top: 3 × 10/arm

2a) Seated Machine Chest Press (or Push-Up): 3 × 12
2b) Lat Pull Down (palms facing your face, shoulder-width
    apart): 3 × 12
2c) Dumbbell Lateral Shoulder Raise: 3 × 12

3a) Cable Rope Biceps Curl: 3 × 15
3b) Cable Rope Triceps Press Down: 3 × 15
3c) Cable Rope Face Pull: 3 × 15

Three Days/Week Workout Program

Mon / Tues / Fri

Day 1: Lower Body and Abs

1a) Sumo Deadlift: 3 × 5
1b) Glute Bridge: 3 × 10

2a) Goblet Squat: 3 × 10
2b) Dumbbell Romanian Deadlift: 3 × 10
2c) Single-Leg Plank: 3 × 15sec/leg

3a) Dumbbell Reverse Lunge: 3 × 12/leg
3b) Leg Curl on Physio Ball: 3 × 12
3c) Bicycle Crunch: 3 × 12/side

Day 2: Upper Body

1a) Dumbbell Bench Press: 3 × 8
1b) Dumbbell Row: 3 × 8/arm

2a) Push-Up: 3 × 10 (elevate your hands if needed)
2b) Batwing Row: 3 × 12
2c) Dumbbell Front Shoulder Raise: 3 × 12

3a) Seated Dumbbell Shoulder Press: 3 × 12
3b) Seated Dumbbell Hammer Curl: 3 × 12/arm
3c) Seated Dumbbell Overhead Triceps Extension: 3 × 12

Day 3: Full Body

1a) Squat: 3 × 6

1b) Seated Alternating Dumbbell Shoulder Press: 3 × 10/arm

2a) Single-Leg Romanian Deadlift: 3 × 8/leg

2b) Seated Machine Chest Press (or Push-Up): 3 × 12

3a) Bulgarian Split Squat: 3 × 8/leg

3b) Lat Pull Down (palms facing your face, shoulder-width apart): 3 × 12

4a) Single-Leg Hip Thrust: 3 × 15/leg

4b) Cable Rope Triceps Press Down: 3 × 15

4c) Russian Twist: 3 × 12/side

Acknowledgments

Many people made this book possible but we especially want to thank:

Our amazing wives for their love and support.

Our parents, thank you from the bottom of our hearts for everything you've done for us.

Our family and friends for their support and encouragement.

Gary Vaynerchuk, who has served many roles from coaching client to business mentor, and now, most important, great friend.

We acknowledge the HarperCollins team, with a special shout-out to our brilliant and tenacious editors, Rebecca and Wendy.

Thank you to every coaching client, every Syatt Fitness Inner Circle member, every person who has downloaded Mike's Macros, and, frankly, to anyone who has read an article, watched a video, hearted a social media post, or listened to a podcast we've put out over the last decade; it is a privilege to do what we do for a living, and without your attention none of this would be possible.

Most important, thank you, God, for the gifts and opportunities you've granted us; without you none of this would be possible.

Appendix: Macros Cheat Sheet

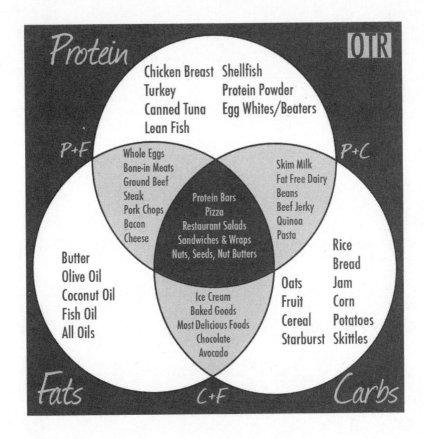

Protein

OTR

Chicken Breast   Shellfish
Turkey   Protein Powder
Canned Tuna   Egg Whites/Beaters
Lean Fish

P+F

Whole Eggs
Bone-in Meats
Ground Beef
Steak
Pork Chops
Bacon
Cheese

Protein Bars
Pizza
Restaurant Salads
Sandwiches & Wraps
Nuts, Seeds, Nut Butters

P+C

Skim Milk
Fat Free Dairy
Beans
Beef Jerky
Quinoa
Pasta

Rice
Bread
Jam
Corn
Potatoes
Skittles

Oats
Fruit
Cereal
Starburst

Butter
Olive Oil
Coconut Oil
Fish Oil
All Oils

Ice Cream
Baked Goods
Most Delicious Foods
Chocolate
Avocado

Fats

C+F

Carbs

Index

About the Authors

JORDAN SYATT and MICHAEL VACANTI are Gary Vayner-chuk's personal trainers. Jordan is the founder of Syatt Fitness, and Mike is the founder of On the Regimen, their respective online fitness coaching businesses. The two have helped hundreds of clients in the gym and thousands more online to get leaner, stronger, and healthier, and to develop a better relationship with food. Mike and Jordan also cohost the *How to Become a Personal Trainer* podcast. Their work has been featured all over the world and across the media, including CNN, *Huffington Post*, *Business Insider*, *Men's Health*, *Men's Fitness*, and more. Jordan lives in Dallas and Mike lives in New York City.